POETRY
AND
JAZZ
IN
CONCERT

POEMS FROM POETRY AND JAZZ IN CONCERT

an anthology edited by
Jeremy Robson

SOUVENIR PRESS LONDON

*For Carole, veteran of 100 concerts,
and for my parents*

© Copyright 1969 introduction and editing of
the selection for this anthology Jeremy Robson

© Copyright 1969 individual poems in this
anthology the authors or their representatives
as shown in the acknowledgements.
All rights reserved

Designed by Felix Gluck

First published 1969 by Souvenir Press
Ltd., 95 Mortimer Street, London, W.1 and
simultaneously by The Ryerson Press,
Toronto 2, Canada

*No part may be reproduced in any form without
permission in writing from the publisher except
for a reviewer who wishes to quote brief
passages for the purposes of a review.*

SBN.285.50240.9

*Printed in Great Britain
by Richard Clay (The Chaucer Press), Ltd.,
Bungay, Suffolk*

CONTENTS

	Introduction	10
Dannie	As I was Saying	16
Abse	Duality	16
	On the Beach	18
	The Water Diviner	20
	A New Diary	21
Thomas	Hospital for Defectives	22
Blackburn	A Small Keen Wind	23
	For a Child	23
	Teaching Wordsworth	24
	Schiara	27
Edwin	Song of the Battery Hen	28
Brock	Betrayal	29
	Incident on the 8.40	30
	Five Ways to Kill a Man	31
Pete Brown	Slam	33
Alan	William Empson at	
Brownjohn	Aldermaston	35
	Go Away	37
	Two Poems after Prévert	38
	The Preservation	41
Michael	Orpheus Street, S.E.5	42
Hamburger	Tides	44
	At Fifty-five	45
	Bird Watcher	47
	S-Bahn	48

John Heath-Stubbs	Epitaph	49
	Use of Personal Pronouns	50
	Titus and Berenice	53
Douglas Hill	Jewish Wedding Ceremony	54
	Sarcophagi in the British Museum	55
	Lighthearted Myth-song	56
	Stranger	57
Anselm Hollo	Man, Animal, Clock of Blood	58
	The Agent	59
Ted Hughes	Out	60
	2nd Bedtime Story	62
	Pike	64
	You Drive in a Circle	65
	Hawk Roosting	66
Bernard Kops	For The Record	68
	Shalom Bomb	69
	Erica I Want to Read You Something	70
Laurie Lee	Stork in Jerez	72
	First Love	73
	April Rise	74
	Day of These Days	74
	The Long War	76

Christopher Logue	Blues Lament	77
	The Song of the Dead Soldier	78
	Go to The Wall	80
Spike Milligan	Ye Tortures	81
	Rain	82
	Porridge	82
Adrian Mitchell	Briefing	83
	Nostalgia—Now Threepence Off	84
	Fifteen Million Plastic Bags	86
Dom Moraes	The Garden	87
	John Nobody	88
	Rendezvous	92
	Snow on a Mountain	93
Peter Porter	Metamorphosis	94
	Annotations of Auschwitz	95
	John Marston Advises Anger	97
	Made in Heaven	98
	Your Attention Please	99
Jeremy Robson	Waking	101
	Just Call	102
	Travelling	103
	Back	105
	Song for a Season	106
Vernon Scannell	Taken in Adultery	107
	An Old Lament Renewed	108

Vernon Scannell	The Men Who Wear My Clothes	110
	No Sense of Direction	110
	I'm Covered Now	112
Jon Silkin	The Cunning of An Age	114
	Sacred	116
	Moss	118
	Astringencies	119
John Smith	Death at The Opera	121
	Day	122
	Would'st Eat a Crocodile	124
	A Florentine Comedy	126
	A Small Consolation	127
Stevie Smith	I Remember	128
	The Jungle Husband	128
	Thoughts about the Person from Porlock	129
	Not Waving but Drowning	131
Nathaniel Tarn	The Life We Do Not Lead	132
	The Cure	133
	The Wedding	134
	The Rights of Man	135
	Biographical Notes	136
	Appendix	140

ACKNOWLEDGEMENTS

For permission to reprint copyright material acknowledgement is made to the following:

For poems by Dannie Abse from *Tenants of The House, Poems, Golders Green*, and *A Small Desperation* (Hutchinson and Co. Ltd.) to the author and Christy and Moore Ltd.; for poems by Thomas Blackburn from *The Next Word, A Smell of Burning*, and *A Breathing Space* to the author and Putnam and Co.; for poems by Edwin Brock from *Penguin Modern Poets No. 8* and *With Love From Judas* to the author and The Scorpion Press; for poems by Pete Brown from *Few* to the author and The Fulcrum Press; for poems by Alan Brownjohn from *The Railings* (Digby Press) and *The Lions' Mouths* to the author and Macmillan and Co. Ltd.; for poems by Michael Hamburger from *Weather and Season* to the author and Messrs. Longmans, Green, and Co. Ltd.; for poems by John Heath-Stubbs from *Selected Poems* (Oxford University Press) to the author and David Highams Associates, Ltd.; for the poem by Anselm Hollo from *Here We Go* (Stranger's Press, 1965 and © Turret Books, 1968) to the author; for poems by Ted Hughes from *Lupercal* and *Wodwo* to Faber and Faber Ltd.; for poems by Bernard Kops from *Erica I Want to Read You Something* to the Scorpion Press; for poems by Laurie Lee from *The Sun My Monument* (Hogarth Press), *Bloom of Candles* (John Lehmann), and *Selected Poems* (Vista Books) to the author and Laurence Pollinger Ltd.; for poems by Christopher Logue from *The Lillywhite Boys, The Man Who Told His Love*, and *Songs* (Hutchinson and Co. Ltd.) to the author and The Scorpion Press; for the poems by Spike Milligan from *The Little Pot Boiler* and *A Dustbin of Milligan* to Dennis Dobson, London; for poems by Adrian Mitchell from *Poems* and *Out Loud* to Jonathan Cape Ltd.; for poems by Dom Moraes from *A Beginning* (Parton Press), *Poems*, and *John Nobody* to the author, John Johnson, and Eyre and Spottiswoode Ltd.; for poems by Peter Porter from *Penguin Modern Poets No. 2* and *Once Bitten, Twice Bitten* to the author and The Scorpion Press; for poems by Vernon Scannell from *A Sense of Danger* and *Walking Wounded* to the author and Eyre and Spottiswoode Ltd.; for poems by Jon Silkin from *The Peaceable Kingdom, The Reordering of the Stones*, and *Nature With Man* to the author and Chatto and Windus Ltd.; for poems by John Smith from *A Discreet Immorality* (Rupert Hart-Davis Ltd.) to the author and Christy and Moore Ltd.; for poems by Stevie Smith from *Selected Poems* to the author and Messrs. Longmans, Green, and Co. Ltd.; for poems by Nathaniel Tarn from *Penguin Modern Poets No. 7*, and *Old Savage/Young City*, to the author and Jonathan Cape Ltd.

All other poems are published with the kind permission of their authors.

INTRODUCTION

The poets represented here have one thing in common. They have all participated—on more than one occasion—in the programmes of Poetry and Jazz in Concert presented by invitation in various parts of the country over the last eight years—for Centre 42, for local authorities and festival committees, for colleges and universities, for individual theatre managements, for the Arts Council, and so on. Many of the poems read by them on these occasions (*without* jazz, I should add) are to be found in this anthology.

Poetry and Jazz in Concert began, rather anarchically, at the Hampstead Town Hall on February 4th, 1961. That first concert surprised audience and participants alike. Four hundred people had to be turned away from the packed Town Hall, and Spike Milligan, who came to read some of his comic verse, was so impressed by the response to the poems read that he urged me to organise a follow-up reading at the Royal Festival Hall. So the second reading took place there on June 11th, 1961, a hot Sunday afternoon. Next day the *Daily Herald* wrote: "The poets went to the Festival Hall yesterday, read their poems ... and *three thousand* people gave them the reception normally reserved for the great names of music. I call that a bit of history."

After the Festival Hall I was invited to organise a Sunday concert at the Belgrade Theatre, Coventry. At the Belgrade, the Michael Garrick Trio, with trumpeter Shake Keane as guest artist, participated for the first time. Arnold Wesker was in the audience and later asked me to arrange a series of concerts for his forthcoming Centre 42 Festivals. Other invitations followed—from Cheltenham, and then from Birmingham and Oxford. Michael Garrick's Trio evolved into a quintet as Shake Keane and

Joe Harriott became regulars. Spike Milligan went to Australia, but the audiences still came. In Cardiff, the "gods" at the Prince of Wales Theatre had to be opened for the first time in years; and at the St. Pancras Arts Festival, 5s. tickets were being hawked for £1.

There have now been several hundred concerts and a number of very different poets have participated. Audiences remain large: about 400 people on average. The concerts, through experience, have naturally assumed a more ordered and purposeful shape than their rough-and-ready beginnings promised: generally, four poets reading, two in each half, with specially written interludes of jazz played as "bridges" between readers—also a few poems read with jazz. (Because the poems written for and read to jazz are necessarily incomplete without their complementary music, I have not included any in this selection.) The poets who read are serious poets, who would certainly eschew the label "pop" and shy away from any form of overt showmanship. They read their own poems, and they read them well: that's all.

The jazz helps, of course. It provides a relaxed and unpretentious atmosphere in which "straight" poetry can be listened to and enjoyed. For the musicians, the advantage is a new and attentive audience. Michael Garrick, the brilliant pianist-composer whose original compositions have contributed greatly to the concerts' success, underlined this point in the *Poetry Review*: "People who love jazz and hate poetry are learning something new: people who like poetry only, begin to find that 'there's something in jazz'. . . . If we've proved nothing else, we have shown that people are not so easily categorised as is often assumed. That this is so is indicated by the unanimous surprise and delight expressed by the poets themselves when they find a warmth of response from poetry and jazz audiences which they had given up long ago like a search for the Holy Grail." Laurie Lee, a regular reader in the early concerts, supports this view: "Those who think that one form detracts from the other," he says, "have 'one-beat minds'."

Dannie Abse, writing in a weekly newspaper, had this to say: "Poetry readings often turn out to be deadly dull. A pious atmosphere somehow suffocates the gathering. Too often it's a snob affair; women in hats dominate except for the superior young man in the front row with a Modigliani neck who stares at the poet with septic hostility. For some time, though, I've engaged in a very different kind of poetry reading. . . . Most of the audiences are young and refreshingly enthusiastic. The atmosphere is far from 'pious' and this allows people to listen to the most quiet and lyrical of poems without feeling ill at ease."

Yet the prejudices remain. Although we have worked for the opposite, the journalist's image of long-haired, ranting, beatnik poets, of beer-spilling, drug-taking, key-pounding musicians, is not easily shaken. Recently, for instance—at the initiative of one student—Dannie Abse, Ted Hughes, and myself were invited with the Garrick quintet to give a concert at a college in the south of England. The authorities were suspicious. On no account could the grand piano in the hall be used: another had to be brought in. Official support of the concert was withheld—until the last minute, when it was realised that people might be coming. The concert was in many ways a triumph. The audience listened intently to the poetry (almost all unaccompanied) and afterwards every book on the table was sold. The principal of the college, who decided at the last moment to attend, exclaimed of the jazz: "Why, it's like chamber music!" It was rehearsed and disciplined, and she was surprised. Afterwards, she bought two jazz records. Do they come for the jazz or the poetry? Here, in part, was the answer. She and other members of the staff had come out of courtesy or duty, but for the poetry mainly. Many of the students had come for the jazz. They heard both. And as John Heath-Stubbs says, "It doesn't matter *why* they come, as long as they come."

There is no doubt that musicians like Michael Garrick, Shake Keane, Joe Harriott, Don Rendell, and Ian Carr[1] (the latter two now feature regularly and brilliantly in the concerts) have their devoted following; that certain poets, too, have their admirers. But it is the curious mixture, the entertainment of contrasts, which often attracts. Whereas poetry readings are "square", poetry and jazz concerts are not: you can take your girl-friend without embarrassment. Mainly, though, it's the creative content of the concerts—the fact that everything read and played is original work, performed by its composer[2]—which generates the excitement frequently lacking in poetry recitals, and which attracts people to come and often to return.

What, from the poets' point of view, have the concerts achieved? Well, they have introduced a cross-section of contemporary poetry to many thousands of people who would otherwise not have encountered it. They have led many to buy books of poems, either at readings, or afterwards at bookshops. This seems to me the most important result—indeed the justification. Poetry readings are an introduction to the written word—or, for those who know the poems, a valuable extension of it—not an end in themselves. Despite the many readings I cannot believe in a "public" or "pop" poetry—only in poetry written for the page, in isolation, with the life and discipline and complexity which good poetry has always possessed. A poet's first commitment, as I see it, is to his poem. If he looks over his shoulder, he's finished. When he's completed the poem, he may choose to read it aloud: but that's another process, another kind of commitment altogether.

[1] *See Appendix.*
[2] *The notable exception is Lydia Pasternak Slater, who participated in some early concerts, reading her translations of her brother Boris' poems.*

This is not to say that reading in public does not affect the poet. John Smith, who has written several groups of poems for the Garrick Quintet, thinks that "reading poetry to a large and miscellaneous audience, and certainly writing poems especially to be read with music, gives a poet a greater awareness of the weight and substance of individual words. It also prevents him from dealing in abstractions." Here we have one obvious side-effect. Poems have been set to, or written for, music. This is not as heretical as some would claim. C. Day Lewis (who has not participated) writes in his book *The Lyric Impulse*: "Unless some poets are willing to experiment with words for music, the lyric impulse as it has been felt for centuries may fade out completely, and the lyric tradition be dead."

Of course there *are* dangers. Dangers to the various poets themselves, that they will develop into performers and writers of verse journalism; that good poets who read badly will be ignored; that bad poets who boom loudly (and topically) may seduce uninitiated audiences into thinking that what they are listening to is typical of contemporary poetry. Orgies of exhibitionism—in or outside the Albert Hall—only do poetry a disservice.

Eight years ago, people laughed; now it's widely accepted that there *is* a public for poetry—if for paperbacks, rather than highly priced slim volumes. This new audience is not easily defined. Certainly many students come to the Poetry and Jazz in Concert programmes, and a good sprinkling of the people who would frequent the Royal Court Theatre, or the Aldwych. These, however (as a writer in *The Guardian* commented), "rarely form half of a typical poetry and jazz audience. The rest is a mixture of young people from shops, offices, factories and (as the *Leicester Mercury* noted after a performance) 'a good stiffening of the middle-aged'." Naturally, the composition of the audience varies. The Centre 42 concerts tended to draw one kind of audience (but not exclusively), universities and colleges draw another, while theatres and art festivals draw from all sections.

For all these words, theory has played little part in the concerts. In choosing poets to read I have tried to be as eclectic as possible and to avoid any kind of grouping: the emphasis has been on complement and contrast throughout. I have invited poets whose work I admire and whose poems—although written for the page—display a certain directness, which enhances their oral appeal. And directness, it seems, depends on a poem having one or more of several qualities, singly or combined: an unashamed lyricism, a comic surface, an evocation of the familiar, a colloquial tone, an urgent contemporary relevance.

The concerts will continue in the future, and I hope that still more poets will take part. It may be immodest, but I do not think it an exaggeration to claim that partly as a result of Poetry and Jazz in Concert, from the Festival Hall onwards, poetry readings, in whatever form, have become a regular and accepted part of the London—and not only the London—scene. Of course, there are some who believe that poetry is for the few. I have never shared this opinion, and it has therefore been most rewarding to witness large audiences responding readily to serious poets reading serious poetry. Rewarding, also, to know that as a result of these readings many have come for the first time to believe that poetry does not belong only to the classroom and the study; that poetry is alive, not entombed; that poetry can amuse, disturb, delight, and enrich.

Many, too, have continued to investigate poetry on the page, long after the chairs have been stacked in the darkened halls. For this reason I am especially grateful for the opportunity to assemble these poems under one, more permanent, roof.

JEREMY ROBSON

Dannie Abse

AS I WAS SAYING

Yes, madam, as a poet I *do* take myself seriously,
and, since I have a young, questioning family, I suppose
I should know something about English wild flowers:
the shape of their leaves, when this and that one grows,
how old mythologies attribute strange powers
to this or that one. Urban, I should mug up anew
the pleasant names: Butterbur, Ling, and Lady's Smock,
Jack-by-the-Hedge, Cuckoo-Pint, and Feverfew,
even the Stinking Hellebore—all in that W. H. Smith book
I could bring home for myself (inscribed to my daughter)
to swot, to know which is this and which that one,
what honours the high cornfield, what the low water,
under the slow-pacing clouds and occasional sun
of England.
 But no! Done for in the ignorant suburb,
I'll drink Scotch, neurotically stare through glass
at the rainy lawn, at green stuff, nameless birds,
and let my daughter, madam, go to nature class.
I'll not compete with those nature poets you advance,
some in country dialect, and some in dialogue
with the country—few as calm as their words:
Wordsworth, Barnes, sad John Clare who ate grass.

DUALITY

Twice upon a time,
there was a man who had two faces,
two faces but one profile:
not Jekyll and Hyde, not good and bad,
and if one were cut, the other would bleed—
two faces different as hot and cold.

Dannie Abse at the Arts Theatre, Cambridge, 1968.
Photo Ilana Steinitz

At night, hung on the hooks on the wall
above that man's minatory head,
one wants brass where one wants gold,
one sees white and one sees black,
and one mouth eats the other
until the second sweet mouth bites back.

They dream their separate dreams
hanging on the wall above the bed.
The first voice cries: "He's not what he seems,"
but the second one sighs: "He is what he is,"
then one shouts "wine" and the other screams "bread",
and so they will all his raving days
until they die on his double-crossed head.

At signposts he must wear them both.
Each would go their separate ways
as the East or the West wind blows—
and dark and light they both would praise,
but one would melt, the other one freeze.

I am that man twice upon this time:
my two voices sing to make one rhyme.
Death I love and Death I hate,
(I'll be with you soon and late).
Love I love, and Love I loathe,
God I mock, and God I prove,
yes, myself I kill, myself I save.

Now, now, I hang these masks on the wall.
Oh Christ, take one and leave me all
lest four tears from two eyes fall.

Michael Garrick (piano) and Coleridge Goode (bass) at the Theatre Royal, Stratford East, 1965. *Photo Ken Coton*

ON THE BEACH

Helen I never went to Troy. Only a phantom went.
Messenger What's this! All that suffering for nothing,
    simply for a cloud?

EURIPIDES *Helena*

Yawning, I fold yesterday's newspaper
from England, and its news of Vietnam
which has had, and will have, a thousand names.
Then I lie back on the tourist sand.

Between the sun and the sea,
far from the sun and nearer to the sea,
a cloud, a single cloud, perhaps
a cloud by Zeus planted,
not much higher than those mountains.
A cloud or a woman's face?

A cloud. Helen never came to Troy.
Mad Paris kissed the pillow where she was not,
straddled the phantom he thought he saw,
and soiling the sheets, lay back still jerking,
"Helen, Helen", satisfied.

I rise. I am level with the haunted sea,
now clear and unclear too deep for wine,
that breathes, because of the cloud, in shadow.
It wrinkles gradually towards me.
Surprise—in the débris of near waves breaking
deluded voices sound within its sound.

As if two, clad like Trojan women,
curse Helen—not sick Paris and his cloud.
For Hector is dead and this one is his mother;
for Hector is dead and that one is his wife,
and his babe, alive, is being torn by beasts.

No camera clicks, no front-page photograph,
no great interview. I laugh aloud,
and hear nearby a transistor braying.
Altered by its dance tune, wrongly I translate:
"Helen, Helen, where are you?
Except for that cloud the sky is blue."

Later, I walk back to the hotel thinking:
wherever women crouch beside their dead,
as Hecuba did, as Andromache,
motionless as sculpture till they raise their head,
with mouths wildly open to howl and curse,
now they call that cloud not Helen, no,
but a thousand names and each one still untrue.

Again I gaze beyond the mountains' range.
In depths below the sun the cloud floats through,
soundless, around the world, it seems, forever.
I go into the hotel, and change.

THE WATER DIVINER

Late, I have come to a parched land
doubting my gift, if gift I have,
the inspiration of water
spilt, swallowed in the sand.

To hear once more water trickle,
to stand in a stretch of silence
the divine pen twisting in the hand:
sign of depths alluvial.

Water owns no permanent shape,
brags, is most itself in chaos;
now, under the shadow of the idol,
dry mouth and dry landscape.

No rain falls with a refreshing sound
to settle tubular in a well,
elliptical in a bowl. No grape
lusciously moulds it round.

Clouds have no constant resemblance
to anything, blown by a hot wind,
flying mirages; the blue background,
light constructions of chance.

To hold back chaos I transformed
amorphous mass: clay, fire, or cloud,
so that the agéd gods might dance
and golden structures form.

I should have built, plain brick on brick,
a water tower. The sun flies on
arid wastes, barren hells too warm,
and me with a hazel stick!

Rivulets vanished in the dust
long ago, great compositions
vaporised, salt on the tongue so thick
that drinking, still I thirst.

Repeated desert, recurring drought,
sometimes hearing water trickle,
sometimes not, I, by doubting first,
believe; believing, doubt.

A NEW DIARY

This clerk-work, this first January chore
of who's in, who's out. A list to think about
when absences seem to shout, Scandal! Outrage!
So turning to the blank, prefatory page
I transfer most of the names and phone tags
from last year's diary. True, Meadway, Speedwell,
Mountview, are computer-changed into numbers,
and already their pretty names begin to fade
like Morwenna, Julie, Don't-Forget-Me-Kate,
grassy summer girls I once swore love to.
These, whispering others and time will date.

Cancelled, too, a couple someone else betrayed,
one man dying, another mind in rags.
And remembering them my clerk-work flags,
bitterly flags, for all lose, no-one wins,
those in, those out, *this* at the heart of things.
So I stop, ask: whom should I commemorate,
and who, perhaps, is crossing out my name
now from some future diary? Oh my God,
Morwenna, Julie, don't forget me, Kate.

Thomas Blackburn

HOSPITAL FOR DEFECTIVES

By your unnumbered charities
A miracle disclose,
Lord of the Images, whose love
The eyelid and the rose
Takes for a language, and today
Tell to me what is said
By these men in a turnip field
And their unleavened bread.

For all things seem to figure out
The stirrings of your heart,
And two men pick the turnips up
And two men pull the cart;
And yet between the four of them
No word is ever said.
Because the yeast was not put in
Which makes the human bread.
But three men stare on vacancy
And one man strokes his knees;
What is the meaning to be found
In such dark vowels as these?

Lord of the Images, whose love
The eyelid and the rose
Takes for a metaphor, today,
Beneath the warder's blows,
The unleavened man did not cry out
Or turn his face away;
Through such men in a turnip field
What is it that you say?

A SMALL KEEN WIND

My wife for six months now in sinister
Tones has muttered incessantly about divorce,
And, since of the woman I'm fond, this dark chatter
Is painful as well as a bit monotonous.
Still, marvel one must, when she fishes out of that trunk,
Like rags, my shadier deeds for all to see
With "This you did when sober, and that when drunk",
At the remarkable powers of memory.
For although I wriggle like mad when she whistles up
Some particularly nasty bit of handiwork,
The dirty linen I simply cannot drop,
Since "Thomas Blackburn" is stitched by the laundry mark.
So I gather the things and say, "Yes, these are mine,
Though some cleaner items are not upon your list",
Then walk with my bundle of rags to another room
Since I will not play the role of delinquent ghost
And be folded up by guilt in the crook of an arm.
I saw tonight—walking to cool the mind—
A little moonshine on a garden wall
And, as I brooded, felt a small, keen wind
Stroll from the Arctic at its own sweet will.

FOR A CHILD

And have I put upon your shoulders then,
What in myself I have refused to bear,
My own and the confusion of dead men,
You of all these, my daughter, made my heir,
The furies and the griefs of which I stayed
Quite unaware?

Perhaps because I did not with my tongue
State these sharp energies into the mind,
They are the shadows you grow up among;
You suffer darkness because I was blind,
Take up the chaosses that in myself
Were unconfined.

If I should say, I also know the tart
Flavour of other men, as my excuse,
And took into myself their broken heart,
That's not the point, abuse remains abuse;
May chaos though have light within your mind,
And be of use.

TEACHING WORDSWORTH

For Alex and Irene Evans

I'm paid to speak, and money glosses
Irrelevance; to keep their places
Students are paid, and so the burden
Is lightened of our mutual boredom,
And if the gain's not much, the damage
Is also slight within this college.

"Since for the most part it's subjective,
Verse is not anything you might have
In hand or a bank, although it is
Important to some (it is on our syllabus)
Concerned with life's outgoing towards death.
Our theme today is the poet, Wordsworth,

"Who, since not alive still, I disinter
For the sake of a question you will answer,
For the sake also of the vagrant lives
He was involved with, and the wind when it raves
Round such unmarketable places as Scawfell.
An unsociable man and often dull,

"He lived for a long time posthumous
To the 'flashing shield', to the poet he was,
Busy for the most part with pedestrian exercise;
However you will not be questioned on those days,
Only the time when with stone footfall
Crags followed him, winds blew through his long skull.

"That, of course, is known as 'the Great Period'.
Though one hesitates to apply the word 'God'
To a poet's theme—it is so manhandled—
Gentlemen, I can offer you nothing instead;
If he himself never applied it to what occurred
When 'the light of sense went out', this useful word
Though inaccurate will cut my lecture short,
Being the full-stop which ends thought

"And consequently for our purpose useful;
For its brevity you should be grateful.
Anyway for those who 'know' what the man meant,
My words are—thanks to God—irrelevant.
'Take notes' is the advice I bequeath the rest;
It is a question of self-interest,

"Of being, as Shakespeare says, 'to oneself true',
Since the right marks will certainly benefit you.
After all, in the teaching world exam and thesis
For the better posts provide a sound basis,

And in this sense poems are as good as money.
This man's life was a strange journey.

"Early deprived of both father and mother,
To the rocks he turned, to lapping water,
With a sense by deprivation made so acute
That he heard grass speak and the word in a stone's throat;
Many, of course, to silence address their prayer,
But in his case when he spoke it chose to answer,

"And he wrote down, after a certain time-lag,
Their conversation. It is a dialogue
Almost unique in any literature
And a positive gold-mine to the commentator,
For although his words mention what silence said
It can almost any way be interpreted,

"Since to find a yardstick by which the occult
Language of stones can be measured is difficult,
Also that 'something far more deeply interfused'
Must be belittled by critiques, if not abused,
There being no instrument with which to measure
This origin of terms and formula

"Which, together with the birth and deathward aim
Of the life in us and things, was this man's theme
As he drew and dwindled into a worse
End of life (as regards verse).
My conclusion is: most words do violence
To what he said. Listen to silence."

SCHIARA[1]

No petal has moved or feather
This day of heat without wind
Of the tamarisk and mimosa
And now they earthward bend
For the catharsis of thunder
That broods and gathers up there
In the cauldron of Schiara,
A potency of fire.

Your head lies on my shoulder,
Sweating because of the heat,
Last night in the dusk from La Stanga
We came to a mountain hut,
And made peace with a hunger
On wine and meat and bread,
Which though it continues forever
Still needs such common good.

Since meeting is knowing, and meeting
Is knowing we understand
So little, under Schiara,
This night of heat but no wind,
For the catharsis of thunder
Wait with me world without end.

[1] *Schiara—mountains in the Italian Dolomites.*

Edwin Brock

SONG OF THE BATTERY HEN

We can't grumble about accommodation:
we have a new concrete floor that's
always dry, four walls that are
painted white, and a sheet-iron roof
the rain drums on. A fan blows warm air
beneath our feet to disperse the smell
of chicken-shit and, on dull days,
fluorescent lighting sees us.

You can tell me: if you come by
the North door, I am in the twelfth pen
on the left-hand side of the third row
from the floor; and in that pen
I am usually the middle one of three.
But, even without directions, you'd
discover me. I have the same orange-
red comb, yellow beak and auburn
feathers, but as the door opens and you
hear above the electric fan a kind of
one-word wail, I am the one
who sounds loudest in my head.

Listen. Outside this house there's an
orchard with small moss-green apple
trees; beyond that, two fields of
cabbages; then, on the far side of
the road, a broiler house. Listen:
one cockerel grows out of there, as
tall and proud as the first hour of sun.
Sometimes I stop calling with the others
to listen, and wonder if he hears me.

The next time you come here, look for me.
Notice the way I sound inside my head.
God made us all quite differently,
and blessed us with this expensive home.

BETRAYAL

Sometime, a long time ago, I
signed a kind of contract.
It was Easter, or some spring
holiday, and I remember the
armfuls of buds that we carried.
It seemed then that we could
live easily in a house full of trees,
she with her brown innocence and
I with a blond assurance.

Over the years our houses took to
trees and our rooms to children;
over the years four voices grew
in unison. And I gave in work
what she would give in love.

I could not understand that
marriages are mortal. Nightly
my key unkocked a kind of blessing
and my limbs looked forward to
our love. At Easter we still
returned bud-laden and out of breath.
Our house grew trees and
our children grew among them.

I see now that gardens are never
quite so certain. I regret the trees
and the serpents that they grew.
This, I should tell myself, is the
only way to God. But, looking back,
I am overcome by the deception of
bright sunlight in a polished room.

INCIDENT ON THE 8.40

He said "I'm going home"

We were between Sydenham
                and Herne Hill.

I lit my third cigarette
and watched the trees go by.

He said "I felt dizzy
at the top of the ladder"

I thought Christ.

He said "I didn't feel well
when I got up this morning"

The sky was blue
and the clouds were full of
                lovesongs.

I thought this is all I need.

He said "My lips feel parched
and my skin's a funny colour"

I said "Yes"
and he said "I'm frightened".

I noticed another tree
and he said "My eyes . . .
there's a pain here . . . and
I can see two of you"

I sang Somewhere Over the Rainbow
and he got off at Herne Hill.

The phantom God of Love
had struck again.

FIVE WAYS TO KILL A MAN

There are many cumbersome ways to kill a man.
You can make him carry a plank of wood
to the top of a hill and nail him to it. To do this
properly you require a crowd of people
wearing sandals, a cock that crows, a cloak
to dissect, a sponge, some vinegar and one
man to hammer the nails home.

Or you can take a length of steel,
shaped and chased in a traditional way,
and attempt to pierce the metal cage he wears.
But for this you need white horses,
English trees, men with bows and arrows,
at least two flags, a prince and a
castle to hold your banquet in.

Dispensing with nobility, you may, if the wind
allows, blow gas at him. But then you need
a mile of mud sliced through with ditches,
not to mention black boots, bomb craters,
more mud, a plague of rats, a dozen songs
and some round hats made of steel.

In an age of aeroplanes, you may fly
miles above your victim and dispose of him by
pressing one small switch. All you then
require is an ocean to separate you, two
systems of government, a nation's scientists,
several factories, a psychopath and
land that no-one needs for several years.

These are, as I began, cumbersome ways
to kill a man. Simpler, direct, and much more neat
is to see that he is living somewhere in the middle
of the twentieth century, and leave him there.

The Quintet at the Institute of Contemporary Arts, 1969: Michael Garrick (piano), Dave Green (bass), Trevor Tomkins (drums), Don Rendell (flute), and Ian Carr (trumpet). *Photo Ken Coton*

Pete Brown

SLAM

They slammed the door
in my face
I opened
the door in my face

My father put me
to bed sneering
Youre a crossbreed
Its true vinegar
was pouring from my ears & nostrils

When I got into bed
the walls swore
hideously all night
& a hidden radio chanted
Rent a chocolate biscuit for
£30 a day
theyre slimy & comfortable!

Halfway through the
night I
went into the garden
& tried to hang
several ants with my bootlace

When I got back
the floor was covered
in bloody maps
& there was a live
octopus in the sink
trying to swallow a
record by Charlie Mingus

Thomas Blackburn at St. Pancras Town Hall, 1966.

I started
sweeping up the
leaves embroidered on
the curtains undismayed
by the savagery next door
Someone hurled a spear
right though the wall
cutting last years calendar in 2

The next step was to
carry the electric stove
around trying to melt
the doorknobs
I achieved this
silently &
soon all the doors
were blazing merrily
Welcome inferno! I
shouted

They found me
in the kitchen
trying to outwhistle
the whistling kettle

In the morning my
mother
had me arrested
by 7
uniformed uncles
named Bloch

Alan Brownjohn

WILLIAM EMPSON AT ALDERMASTON

This is our dead sea, once a guidebook heath.
Left and right hands worked busily together
A parliament or two,
And there she stands:

Twelve miles of cooling pipes; concrete and secret
Warrens underground; clean little towers
Clamped with strong ladders; red, brisk vans
Which hurry round

The wide, kerbed avenues with pulsing lights
To signify danger; and all this
Extending still its miles, as seas possessed
Of power or anger

Will—except that here
The tide decrees, with threats in yellow paint,
Its own unquestioned bounds, keeps dogs to catch
Someone who gets

Beyond the fence: it seems that otherwise
We shiver from an unclean nakedness,
And need to clothe our hot emotions cold
With wire, and curs.

But let there be some praise, where that is due:
For paint, of enlivening colours, spent
On all these deathly offices. Where typists sit,
Who do not make the thing,

Or scientists, who do not fire the thing,
Or workers, who obey the scientists,
The rooms are beautiful. And anyone
Who passed by car one day

Not knowing what it was would never guess.
(Perhaps some urgent public undertaking
Set up for health, or water? Or a camp
Where other people went

On holidays?) Such airs of carnival,
With death designed as smiling, to conceal
His proper features—these things justified
Replies in kind:

An absurd fête of life, in one Friday field
For which no pass was needed. The effect:
Two sorts of carnival clashing: on this side
The mud, or grass,

The boots and stoves and caravans; that side,
The trim, discreet pavilions of the State.
And one more contrast marked these gaieties:
This side there seemed

Some thousands, while of death's there wasn't one.
Just the white-braided police returned the stare
Of the boys with haversacks, or the fierce
Empirical gaze

Of the man with the Chinese beard, or the pondering glance
Of the woman with the basket on wheels.
And some thought death's precise executives
Had told or asked

The servants of his will to stay away,
Hinting of jobs they might not like to lose,
And they had houses . . . from whose windows, next,
Many faces looked the way

Of the procession: speaking not a word,
But merely watching. How else, then, explain
If this was not the reason, why their children,
Through all the bands and singing,

All the beards and the guitars, did not come out;
But stood behind held curtains, listlessly,
With tight and puzzled faces, or peered through
Some furtive upstairs sunblind

While it passed? No coloured hat, not one
In all the range of shirts and slogans worn,
Seemed odder than these faces. That deep blankness
Was the real thing strange.

GO AWAY

I have come about the ground, is this your ground?
—Go away, I want to kneel by myself
On this first dry patch of the year, and prepare the soil.

That's a right occupation, but my purpose is to warn you
About the ground—Look, a person like me
Has no time to talk. I've only one evening for the garden.

But please, I think your ground may not be safe!
—Yes, but don't come and bother me now. I have bulbs
Which I want to settle in; and there are pebbles to sift out.

Listen, someone is deliberately undermining your garden
—You are worse than the weeds and the greenfly. Go away.
When shall I get these narcissi planted?

But even if you plant them they won't grow. They won't have
Any time to sprout or flower.
—But I've always grown flowers here. Why say things like that?

*Because the ground is undermined, they are going
To blow it up.*—What you're saying is ridiculous.
I trust them. I know they would never do such a thing.

Then who are those men bending down at the edge of the garden,
What is this spreading tremor of the ground
That snatches the spade from your hand?

What is wrenching the saplings up?—Why expect me to know?
I suppose they must know what they are doing.
I suppose it's for the best. Why don't you go away!

TWO POEMS AFTER PRÉVERT

I

In this city, perhaps a street.
In this street, perhaps a house.
In this house, perhaps a room
And in this room a woman sitting,
Sitting in the darkness, sitting and crying
For someone who had just gone through the door
And who has just switched off the light
Forgetting she was there.

II
We are going to see the rabbit.
We are going to see the rabbit.
Which rabbit, people say?
Which rabbit, ask the children?
Which rabbit?
The only rabbit,
The only rabbit in England,
Sitting behind a barbed-wire fence
Under the floodlights, neon lights,
Sodium lights,
Nibbling grass
On the only patch of grass
In England, in England
(Except the grass by the hoardings
Which doesn't count).
We are going to see the rabbit
And we must be there on time.

First we shall go by escalator,
Then we shall go by underground,
And then we shall go by motorway
And then by helicopterway,
And the last ten yards we shall have to go
On foot.
And now we are going
All the way to see the rabbit.
We are nearly there,
We are longing to see it,
And so is the crowd
Which is here in thousands
With mounted policemen
And big loudspeakers
And bands and banners,
And everyone has come a long way.

But soon we shall see it
Sitting and nibbling
The blades of grass
On the only patch of grass
In—but something has gone wrong!
Why is everyone so angry,
Why is everyone jostling
And slanging and complaining?

The rabbit has gone,
Yes, the rabbit has gone.
He has actually burrowed down into the earth
And made himself a warren, under the earth,
Despite all these people.
And what shall we do?
What *can* we do?

It is all a pity, you must be disappointed,
Go home and do something else for today,
Go home again, go home for today.
For you cannot hear the rabbit, under the earth,
Remarking rather sadly to himself, by himself,
As he rests in his warren, under the earth:
"It won't be long, they are bound to come,
They are bound to come and find me, even here."

THE PRESERVATION

It's quite worth keeping your surprise at the untrodden
Snow on the long step that particular winter night
—As if we had been indoors for days—

As in that time your every movement told,
And looked responsible. Never had your feet
Set out their marks on things with such grave care,

Or honour of any place. And all the mocking
Extensions to words in your hands' actions
Drained right away, or were absolved

In one cupped, simple gesture, collecting
(To taste and to smile) some snow in a quick mild heap
From the near top of the street wall.

Michael Hamburger

ORPHEUS STREET, S.E.5

1

Will they move, will they dance,
These houses put up by the money-makers
For the meek, their no-men, to breed in,
Breed money dispersed now, decayed?
And the pawn shop, government surplus,
The cut price petrol station,
Dirty brick, waste paper,
Will his music gather them up?

2

Orpheus transfigures, Orpheus transmutes all things.
His music melts walls. His music wrings
A smile from the lips of killer and nearly killed.
He wills pavements to crack. He whistles at trains,
They whimper, gasp and give up. Wherever "it" sings
It is Orpheus—with it, well paid for his pains.
Grow, says Orpheus, and dog collars burst,
Tall factories shiver, the whole town swings.

3

Oh, but the traffic diversions.
The road marked World's End, The West,
Runs north and east and south,
And the policeman on duty sneers:
Never mind the direction. You'll get there.
Be courteous. Be patient. If you park
Your car will be towed away.
If you walk, louts will kick in your ribs.

4

Orpheus is peaceable. Orpheus is faithful
To the woman who was his wife,
Till she suffered a blackout, going

Down, down, where he couldn't reach her,
Where no one belongs to himself,
Far less to another. He lost her;
But loves her still, and loves everyone,
Richly paid for loving.

5
They shriek, they sob for Orpheus,
For a shred of his shirt or flesh.
He turns right, then left,
Proceeds, does a U-turn,
Turns left, turns right, turns left,
The shriek in his ears, everywhere.
He swallows a capsule, prepares
A love song, a peace song, a freedom song.

6
The smile on her face, her smile
When he questioned her eyes for the last time
And she walked away from the stranger.
In halflight he sees no warehouse
But chasms, a river, rock.
A last glint on her hair
And the cave's darkness takes her,
Silent. Silent he leaves.

7
Let lamp posts be trees for once,
Bend their trunks, the park benches
Fling out their limbs, let them fly,
Narrowly missing the sparrows.
Street and mind will not meet
Till street and mind go down
And the footfall that faded, faded,
Draws closer again in the dark.

8

Lamplit or moonlit, his deathland:
Chasms, a river, rock.
The cries of children in alleyways,
The cries of birds in the air,
And the talons, innocent, tearing.
A head will float on foul water
And sing for the rubble, for her,
For the stars, for empty space.

TIDES

To wake without fail when milk bottles shake in their racks,
Scrape one's face in the morning, every morning,
Take the same route to work and say "good morning"
To the same row of scraped or powdered faces—
I cursed the roundness of this earth, I raged
At every self-perpetuating motion,
Hated the sea, that basher of dumb rock,
For all her factory of weeds and fishes,
The thumps, the thuds, the great reverberations—
Too much in rhythm; jarring, but by rote.

The metronome it was in my own head
That ticked and ticked; caged cricket in my head
That chirped and chirped until I had no ear
For syncopation, counterpoint of stillness
Beating against all music—of the sea,
Of birds and men, of season and machine,
Even of cricket and of metronome.
In silence I learned to listen; in the dark to look.

And unrepeatable now each morning's light
Modulates, shuffles, probes the daily faces
Often too suddenly different, like the street,
This weathered wall re-pointed, that new one cracked,
Apple trees that I prune while I forget
The shape of last year's boughs, cankered or grown,
And where that stump is, one that died in blossom;
Forget the hill's curve under the aerial masts.

No, wheels, grind on; seasons, repeat yourselves;
Milk bottles, rattle; familiars, gabble "good morning";
Breed, hatch, digest your weeds and fishes, sea,
Omit no beat, nor rise to tidal waves.
Various enough the silences cut in
Between the rock cave's boom and the small wader's cry.

AT FIFTY-FIVE

Country dances
Bird calls
The breathing of leaves after thunder—
And now fugues.
Modulations "impolite"
Syncopations "unnatural".
No more clapping of hands
When moonshine had opened their tear-ducts
Or fanfares clenched
Heroic nerves—
But a shaking of heads:
Can't help it, our decomposer,
Can't hear his own blundering discords.

As if one needed ears
For anything but chit-chat about the weather,
Exchange of solicitude, malice—
And birdsong, true, the grosser, the bouncing rhythms.
Uncommunicative? Yes. Unable
"Like beginners to learn from nightingales".
Unwilling, too, for that matter—
To perform, to rehearse, to repeat,
To take in, to give back.

In time out of time, in the concert no longer concerted.
But the music all there, what music,
Where from—
Water that wells from gravel washed clean by water.
All there—inaudible thrushes
Outsinging the nightingales, peasants
Dancing weightless, without their shoes—
Where from, by what virtue? None.
By what grace but still being here, growing older?
The water cleansed by gravel washed clean by water.

Fugue, ever itself—
And ever growing,
Gathering up—itself,
Plunging—into itself,
Rising—out of itself,
Fathoming—only itself
To end, not to end its flowing—
No longer itself—
In a stillness that never was.

BIRD WATCHER

Challenged, he'd say it was a mode of knowing—
As boys in railway stations neutralise a passion
By gathering ciphers: number, date and place—
Yet keeps no record of his rare encounters,
Darkly aware that like his opposite
Who no less deep in woods, as far out on the moors
Makes do with food and trophies, hunts for easy favours,
He trysts defeat by what he cannot know.

"Goldfinch" he says, and means a chirping flutter
From stalk to stalk in early autumn meadows,
Or "oystercatcher", meaning a high, thin cry
More ghost than bodied voice, articulation
Of the last rock's complaint against the sea.

And wooing with his mind the winter fieldfares
Has made a snare of his binoculars,
For lime and cage and gun has longed in secret,
To kill that he may count, ravish despair
And eat the tongue that will not speak to him,
Though to the wind it speaks, evasive as the wind.

He grows no lighter, they no heavier
As to his mode of loving he returns,
Fixed in the discipline of adoration;
Will keep no pigeons, nor be satisfied
With metropolitan starlings garbling their parodies.

The boy's cold bride will yield, too soon and utterly,
Never these engines fuelled with warm blood,
Graced with peculiar folly that will far outfly him
Till in one communal emptiness they meet.

S–BAHN
(Berlin, 1965)

The gunpowder smell,
The corpses have been disposed of,
The gas rose up, diffused.
Kaiser, President, Führer
Have come and gone,
The housewives in funny hats
Came from the suburbs to shop,
Came from the central flats
To litter the woods and lakes,
Gushing about "Natur".
What remains is the carriage smell,
Tobacco smoke and heaters in stale air,
Indefinable, changeless
Monkey-house odour
Heavy on seats as hard
But emptier

Now that the train connects
One desolation with another,
Punctual as ever moves through the rubble
Of Kaiser, President, Führer,
Is halted, searched and cleared
Of those it would serve too well
This winter when, signalled on, it crosses
The frontier, no man's land,
Carrying only the smell
Over to neon lights
Past the deeper snow
Around dead financiers' villas
And the pine-woods' darkness
Into the terminus
Where one foreigner stamps cold feet.

John Heath-Stubbs

EPITAPH

Mr. Heath-Stubbs as you must understand
Came of a gentleman's family out of Staffordshire
Of as good blood as any in England
But he was wall-eyed and his legs too spare.

His elbows and finger-joints could bend more ways than one
And in frosty weather would creak audibly
As to delight his friends he would give demonstration
Which he might have done in public for a small fee.

Amongst the more learned persons of his time
Having had his schooling in the University of Oxford
In Anglo-Saxon Latin ornithology and crime
Yet after four years he was finally not preferred.

Orthodox in beliefs as following the English Church
Barring some heresies he would have for recreation
Yet too often left these sound principles (as I am told) in the lurch
Being troubled with idleness, lechery, pride and dissipation.

In his youth he would compose poems in prose and verse
In a classical romantic manner which was pastoral
To which the best judges of the Age were not averse
And the public also but his profit was not financial.

Now having outlived his friends and most of his reputation
He is content to take his rest under these stones and grass
Not expecting but hoping that the Resurrection
Will not catch him unawares whenever it takes place.

USE OF PERSONAL PRONOUNS:
A LESSON IN ENGLISH GRAMMAR

I

I is at the centre of the lyric poem,
And only there not arrogant.

"You begin every sentence with *I*"—the rebuke was well taken:
But how on earth else am I to begin them?

You and Thou

You are a secret *thou*.
Fumbling amongst the devalued currency
Of "dear" and "darling" and "my love"
I do not dare to employ it—

Not even in a poem, not even
If I were a Quaker, any more.

Beginning as an honorific the unaffectionate *you*,
For English speakers, has put *thou* out of business.
So, in our intimate moments,
We are dumb, in a castle of reserve.

And He alone
From Whom no secrets are hid, to Whom
All hearts be open,
Can be a public *Thou*.

He, She, and It

Only in the third person sex raises its
Unattractive—well, "head" is a fair enough euphemism.
The thought of sex in which you and I
Do not participate is (unless we are *voyeurs*)
Either horrifying or ridiculous. He and she
He it and she it.

But, moving outside the human order,
We observe there is no personality
Apart from gender. Animals are *it*,
But our own cats, horses, and dogs are *he* or *she*;
The huntsman's Puss is *she*, Reynard is *he*;
And even ships are beloved as *she*,
Cars and bicycles, even.

For the homosexual queening it in the Gimcrack Bar
His colleagues, objects of his scandal, are *she*,
While the inaccessible youth in the tight jeans,
Three buttons undone in his scarlet shirt,
Is, however, an *it*.

One

One thinks of *one* as a pronoun employed principally
At Cambridge, modestly to include oneself
And other people in one's own set,
At Cambridge. One appreciates the French usage
Of *on*; one knows one's Henry James;
One does feel (or, of course, alternatively, one does not)
One must, on the whole, concur with Dr. Leavis
(or, of course, alternatively, with Mr. Rylands).
At Oxford, on the other hand,
One tends to become *we*. At Cambridge
One senses a certain arrogance in the Oxford *we*;
A certain exclusiveness in the Cambridge *one*
Is suspected, at Oxford.

We

"We," said Queen Victoria, "are not amused."
Subsuming the entire dinner-table into the impersonal
And royal *We*:
No wonder the effect was devastating.

We is also the Editor of *The Times*
While a Greek chorus is a pattern of dancing *I's*;
The Christian congregation is *I* in the Creed,
Thou in each of the sacraments,
Otherwise solidly *we*. And
"Let Us make man in Our own image."

We is not amused, nor is it interested
In the possibilities of defeat.

They

They is the hellish enemy of paranoiacs
(And even of Auden and Edward Lear);
They is in a conspiracy, is directing hostile thought-waves,—
Has got everything fixed *their* way. *They* will not let you.

History a deadly and unending struggle
Of class and national *theys*, except when sometimes
An imperial and oecumenical *We* serenely
Frowns at a barbarian and utter *they*.

But for you and for me
Weeping in our tragic citadel, the horror
Is simply to realise that *they* exist.

TITUS AND BERENICE

"Turn to me in the darkness,
  Asia with your cool
Gardens beyond the desert,
  Your clear, frog-haunted pool;
I seek your reassurance—
  Forget, as I would forget,
Your holy city cast down, the Temple
  That still I desecrate."
"*Buzz!*" *said the blue-fly in his head.*

"In darkness master me,
  Rome with your seven hills,
Roads, rhetorical aqueducts,
  And ravaging eagles;
Worlds are at bitter odds, yet we
  Can find our love at least—
Not expedient to the Senate,
  Abominable to the priest."
"*Buzz!*" *said the blue-fly in his head.*

Titus the clement Emperor
  And she of Herod's house
Slobbered and clawed each other
  Like creatures of the stews;
Lay together, then lay apart
  And knew they had not subdued—
She the insect in his brain,
  Nor he her angry God.

NOTE. *According to a Jewish tradition Titus was afflicted with an insect in his brain as a punishment for his destruction of the Temple.*

Douglas Hill

JEWISH WEDDING CEREMONY

for J. and C.

Magic in the hand that holds the ring
utters itself—mingling with the light
that focuses the consecration,

flowing from hands as the hymn flows
through the arched spaces of the synagogue
circling within its broader circle

voices transforming word into song,
chant into conception—word
and world new-conceived, new-born

as on sabbath days when heads are bowed
born naked and new like the lives reflected
in sunlight on the goblet's splinters:

Two lives ringed with the music of marriage
who resurrect the words from dust
the ancient ceremonial magic become flesh

Stand forth, the world is remade—
the twofold circle contracts and binds,
with song and sun and sacrament:

Magic in the hand that wears the ring

SARCOPHAGI IN THE BRITISH MUSEUM

One of this temple's galleries
is echoing with death.
Dry brown bags of human skin

scraped from the anonymous
Egyptian sand lie mortified,
exposed. Sure of our disbelief

in *ba*-souls, or their afterlife
lost if the tombs are plundered,
we have caused these cadavers to die

twice. Like Thomas Browne, who feared
exhumation as we fear burial alive
yet whom some curator pried

from his tight grave, to flaunt
his skull in a glass museum case
where it must have screamed for years.

So these husks scream, in an obscene
archaeological peepshow
and the ancient curse on desecrators

falls impotent now as the flesh
flaking on their wrinkled loins
mortified, exposed.

LIGHTHEARTED MYTH-SONG

I wear high boots to go out in the garden
And tight rubber gloves
      (sing to the marigolds)
Point my umbrella in all directions
In case it rains earth
      (sing to the concrete marigolds)

I take my dark glasses out in the garden
To soften the sky
      (laugh at the bluejays)
Handle a parasol, shoulder a shade
Draw the sun's limits
      (laugh at the concrete bluejays)

I button my collar when out in the garden
Keep my lips closed
      (dance on the pathways)
Pass unperturbed by the goat-hairs caught
On the plum tree thorn
      (dance alone
        on the concrete pathways)

STRANGER

One night the man in the room across
the street pulled his curtains
aside and I saw a pink
coverlet on his bed and a naked
wall behind
        The record players next door
to him stay on all night and winter
long on into the spring
        Does
the man in the room over there
lying under his coverlet hear them
and close his eyes against the bareness
of his nights?
        or can he keep
the curtains closed and in subdued light
hear nothing but a surrounding rose cocoon
in $33\frac{1}{3}$ revolutions per lifetime

and need not knock on the unmarked
partition

Anselm Hollo

MAN, ANIMAL, CLOCK OF BLOOD

The animal runs
it eats, it sleeps
it dies
     goes the old song

and then:
the great cold
the night, the dark . . .

In the dark, the man runs
he stumbles, he hurts
  his face, the world is hard on his face, is a she
he is in love with the world

lord of creation, he wears his shoes large
    make way, make way
he does not think of that night
he is warm, he will love her, if only, whenever
    he finds her

if only he could go without eating
if only he could do without sleep
if only he could hold her forever
he need not die
          goes the old song
          in his head

and he keeps on walking & wanting
the beautiful goof, walking and
wanting: make way for the lord
idiot, flower, awkward
                  man

THE AGENT

1

he's watching him
across the sleeping big black desk

there's a slow hum in the air
as they sit there
dangerous

discussing the latest
in the world
around that room

2

sent out on a mission
the thought of that constant
the dark hum reassures him

he braves the cars in the street
the poison green lights
the bombs that whisper through the evening air

the street corner women who look and feel
like shapely containers of chloroform
the men with guns bulging behind their eyes

the big black desk
is humming humming in his heart

3

he has come back
he is heading back to the room

long corridors whistling sound as he passes
an invisible line runs crackles along the ceiling
keeping the pace
the telephones have gone mute lost voices
boys like shadows rise in the doorways
their eyes invisible white
he is heading back to the room

Ted Hughes

OUT

I

The Dream Time

My father sat in his chair recovering
From the four-year mastication by gunfire and mud,
Body buffeted wordless, estranged by long soaking
In the colours of mutilation.
                              His outer perforations
Were valiantly healed, but he and the hearth-fire, its blood-flicker
On biscuit-bowl and piano and table-leg,
Moved into strong and stronger possession
Of minute after minute, as the clock's tiny cog
Laboured and on the thread of his listening
Dragged him bodily from under
The mortised four-year strata of dead Englishmen
He belonged with. He felt his limbs clearing
With every slight, gingerish movement. While I, small and four,
Lay on the carpet as his luckless double,
His memory's buried, immovable anchor,
Among jawbones and blown-off boots, tree-stumps, shell-cases and craters,
Under rain that goes on drumming its rods and thickening
Its kingdom, which the sun had abandoned, and where nobody
Can ever again move from shelter.

II

The dead man in his cave beginning to sweat;
The melting bronze visor of flesh
Of the mother in the baby-furnace——
Nobody believes, it
Could be nothing, all

Undergo smiling at
The lulling of blood in
Their ears, their ears, their ears, their eyes
Are only drops of water and even the dead man suddenly
Sits up and sneezes—Atishoo!
Then the nurse wraps him up, smiling,
And, though faintly, the mother is smiling,
And it's just another baby.

As after being blasted to bits
The reassembled infantryman
Tentatively totters out, gazing around with the eyes
Of an exhausted clerk.

III

Remembrance Day

The poppy is a wound, the poppy is the mouth
Of the grave, maybe of the womb searching—

A canvas-beauty puppet on a wire
Today whoring everywhere. It is years since I wore one.

It is more years
The shrapnel that shattered my father's paybook

Gripped me, and all his dead
Gripped him to a time

He no more than they could outgrow, but, cast into one, like
                                                          iron,
Hung deeper than refreshing of ploughs

In the woe-dark under my mother's eye—
One anchor

Holding my juvenile neck bowed to the dunkings of the Atlantic.
So goodbye to that bloody-minded flower.

You dead bury your dead.
Goodbye to the cenotaphs on my mother's breasts.

Goodbye to all the remaindered charms of my father's survival.
Let England close. Let the green sea-anemone close.

2ND BEDTIME STORY

He loved her and she loved him
His kisses sucked out her whole past and future or tried to
He had no other appetite
She bit him she gnawed him she sucked
She wanted him complete inside her
Safe and sure forever and ever
Their little cries fluttered into the curtains
Her eyes wanted nothing to get away
Her looks nailed down his hands his wrists his elbows
He gripped her hard so that life
Should not drag her from that moment
He wanted all future to cease
He wanted to topple with his arms round her
Off that moment's brink and into nothing
Or everlasting or whatever there was
Her embrace was an immense press
To print him into her bones
His smiles were the garrets of a fairy palace
Where the real world would never come
Her smiles were spider bites
So he would lie still till she felt hungry

His words were occupying armies
Her laughs were an assassin's attempts
His looks were bullets daggers of revenge
Her glances were ghosts in the corner with horrible secrets
His whispers were whips and jackboots
Her kisses were lawyers steadily writing
His caresses were the last hooks of a castaway
Her love-tricks were the grinding of locks
And their deep cries crawled over the floors
Like an animal dragging a great trap
His promises were the surgeon's gag
Her promises took the top off his skull
She would get a brooch made of it
His vows pulled out all her sinews
He showed her how to make a love-knot
Her vows put his eyes in formalin
At the back of her secret drawer
Their screams stuck in the wall,
Their heads fell apart into sleep like the two halves
Of a lopped melon, but love is hard to stop

In their entwined sleep they exchanged arms and legs
In their dreams their brains took each other hostage

In the morning they wore each other's face

PIKE

Pike, three inches long, perfect
Pike in all parts, green tigering the gold.
Killers from the egg: the malevolent aged grin.
They dance on the surface among the flies.

Or move, stunned by their own grandeur,
Over a bed of emerald, silhouette
Of submarine delicacy and horror.
A hundred feet long in their world.

In ponds, under the heat-struck lily pads—
Gloom of their stillness:
Logged on last year's black leaves, watching upwards.
Or hung in an amber cavern of weeds

The jaws' hooked clamp and fangs
Not to be changed at this date;
A life subdued to its instrument;
The gills kneading quietly, and the pectorals.

Three we kept behind glass,
Jungled in weed: three inches, four,
And four and a half: fed fry to them—
Suddenly there were two. Finally one

With a sag belly and the grin it was born with.
And indeed they spare nobody.
Two, six pounds each, over two feet long,
High and dry and dead in the willow-herb—

Upper: Douglas Hill at Hereford College, 1968. *Photo Richard Lake*
Lower: Bernard Kops at the Centre 42 Festival, Leicester, 1962.
Photo John Hopkins

One jammed past its gills down the other's gullet:
The outside eye stared: as a vice locks—
The same iron in this eye
Though its film shrank in death.

A pond I fished, fifty yards across,
Whose lilies and muscular tench
Had outlasted every visible stone
Of the monastery that planted them—

Stilled legendary depth:
It was as deep as England. It held
Pike too immense to stir, so immense and old
That past nightfall I dared not cast

But silently cast and fished
With the hair frozen on my head
For what might move, for what eye might move.
The still splashes on the dark pond,

Owls hushing the floating woods
Frail on my ear against the dream
Darkness beneath night's darkness had freed,
That rose slowly towards me, watching.

YOU DRIVE IN A CIRCLE

Slowly a hundred miles through the powerful rain.

Your clothes are towelled with sweat and the car-glass sweats,
And there is a smell of damp dog.
Rain-sog is rotting your shoes to paper.

Ted Hughes at the Theatre Royal, Stratford East, 1965.
Photo Ken Coton

Over old hairy moors, a dark Arctic depth, cresting under rain,
Where the road topples, plunging with its crazed rigging
Like a rackety iron tanker

Into a lunge of spray, emerges again—
Through hard rendings of water,
Drowned eyes at the melting windshield,

Out above the swamped moor-wallows, the mist-gulfs of no-thinking.
Down in there are the sheep, rooted like sponges,
Chewing and digesting and undeterred.

What could they lose, however utterly they drowned?
Already sodden as they are with the world, like fossils.
And what is not the world is God, a starry comforter of good blood.

Where are you heading? Everything is already here.
Your hardest look cannot anchor out among these rocks,
    your coming days cannot anchor among these torn clouds
    that cannot anchor.

Your destination waits where you left it.

HAWK ROOSTING

I sit in the top of the wood, my eyes closed.
Inaction, no falsifying dream
Between my hooked head and hooked feet:
Or in sleep rehearse perfect kills and eat.

The convenience of the high trees!
The air's buoyancy and the sun's ray
Are of advantage to me;
And the earth's face upward for my inspection.

My feet are locked upon the rough bark.
It took the whole of Creation
To produce my foot, my each feather:
Now I hold Creation in my foot

Or fly up, and revolve it all slowly—
I kill where I please because it is all mine.
There is no sophistry in my body:
My manners are tearing off heads—

The allotment of death.
For the one path of my flight is direct
Through the bones of the living.
No arguments assert my right:

The sun is behind me.
Nothing has changed since I began.
My eye has permitted no change.
I am going to keep things like this.

Bernard Kops

FOR THE RECORD

They came for him in Amsterdam; my grandfather David,
and with minimum force removed him from his house.

He surrendered to the entire German Army,
and that was that.

It is of little consequence now;
so many die alone in foreign lands.
But for the record I must say
they gave him a number, helped him
aboard an east-bound train.
It was a little overcrowded,
but then again they had so many to dispatch.

You might call him part of the biggest catch
in history of those who fish for men.

Anyway, to cut a long story short,
he was never seen again.

I cannot put my finger on the exact day he died.
Nor the time, nor the place.

Suffice to say it was by gas and in the east.

I write this merely to record the facts
for my descending strangers.

Furthermore, today is the 21st of December
in the year of our Lord (Lord?) 1968.
And it is getting rather late.
It rained this evening but now the wind has dropped
and the moon is shining.
It is 11.33 p.m. Precisely.

SHALOM BOMB

I want a bomb, my own private bomb, my shalom bomb.
I'll test it in the morning, when my son awakes,
hot and stretching, smelling beautiful from sleep. Boom! Boom!

Come my son dance naked in the room.
I'll test it on the landing and wake my neighbours,
the masons and the whores and the students who live downstairs.

Oh I must have a bomb and I'll throw open windows and
count down as I whizz around the living room,
on his bike, with him flying angels on my shoulder;
and my wife dancing in her dressing gown.
I want a happy family bomb, a do-it-yourself bomb,
I'll climb on the roof and ignite it there about noon.
My improved design will gong the world and we'll all eat lunch.

My pretty little bomb will play a daytime lullaby and
thank you bomb for now my son falls fast asleep.
My love come close, close the curtains, my lovely bomb, my
 darling.
My naughty bomb. Burst around us, burst between us, burst
 within us.
Light up the universe, then linger, linger
while the drone of the world recedes.

Shalom bomb.

I want to explode the breasts of my wife
and wake everyone,
to explode over playgrounds and parks, just as children

come from schools. I want a laughter bomb,
filled with sherbert fountains, licorice allsorts, chocolate kisses, candy floss,
tinsel and streamers, balloons and fireworks, lucky bags,
bubbles and masks and false noses.
I want my bomb to sprinkle the earth with roses.
I want a one-man-band bomb. My own bomb.

My live long and die happy bomb. My die peacefully of old age bomb,
in my own bed bomb.
My Om Mane Padme Aum Bomb, My Tiddly Om Pom Bomb.
My goodnight bomb, my sleeptight bomb,
my see you in the morning bomb.
I want my bomb, my own private bomb, my Shalom bomb.

ERICA I WANT TO READ YOU SOMETHING

Annihilation is easier when you are lonely.
But a man who is past it,
who knows no hope, who fears,
who fears there is no reason,
is known to me.

That man knows no order, no purpose,
but only knows a casual shape that has become
familiar.
Yet that man does not sing through me.

It all ends in death.
But when you love someone or detach yourself
from your own sadness,
this loss of life is more felt.

When you have a wife in bed,
a wife warm and passionate and beautiful,
when you are in her and she in you
completely,
when your shadows and personalities merge,
what then?

What of the coming loss, one way or another?

Or can the shape of infinite endlessness
bring a sort of tranquil beauty,
that makes you accept and nicely shrug
and sadly, sweetly smile?
Will I smile? Or will she?
Or will universal destruction take us both
together?
Then we will never have to face the lonely end.
Maybe this is why we want to blow ourselves
to kingdom come.

Oh my love, we must pass on some love.

And so we loved within these sheets,
where I sit within this familiar room,
under this universe; writing this.

Now she sleeps, lost in a book.
I will soon call her name, so as not to be
so lonely. And I shall say Erica
I want to read you something.
I shall call her name and this night will pass;
and so will so many,
and this world will pass and so will so many.
ERICA I WANT TO READ YOU SOMETHING.

Laurie Lee

STORK IN JEREZ

White-arched in loops of silence, the bodega
Lies drowsed in spices, where the antique woods
Piled in solera, dripping years of flavour,
Distil their golden fumes among the shades.

In from the yard—where barrels under figtrees
Split staves of sunlight from the noon's hot glare—
The tall stork comes; black-stilted, sagely-witted,
Wiping his careful beak upon the air.

He is a priest-like presence, he inscribes
Sharp as a pen his staid and written dance,
Skating the floor with stiffened plumes behind him,
Gravely off-balance, solemn in his trance.

Drunk on these sherry vapours, eyes akimbo,
He treads among the casks, makes a small leap,
Flaps wildly, fails to fly—until at last,
Folded umbrella-wise, he falls asleep.

So bird and bard exchange their spheres of pleasure:
He, from his high-roofed nest now levelled lies;
Whilst I, earth-tied, breathing these wines take wing
And float amazed across his feathered skies.

FIRST LOVE

That was her beginning, an apparition
of rose in the unbreathed airs of his love,
her heart revealed by the wash of summer
sprung from her childhood's shallow stream.

Then it was that she put up her hair,
inscribed her eyes with a look of grief,
while her limbs grew as curious as coral branches,
her breast full of secrets.

But the boy, confused in his day's desire,
was searching for herons, his fingers bathed
in the green of walnuts, or watching at night
the Great Bear spin from the maypole star.

It was then that he paused in the death of a game,
felt the hook of her hair on his swimming throat,
saw her mouth at large in the dark river
flushed like a salmon.

But he covered his face and hid his joy
in a wild-goose web of false directions,
and hunted the woods for eggs and glow-worms,
for rabbits tasteless as moss.

And she walked in fields where the crocuses
branded her feet, and mares' tails sprang
from the prancing lake, and the salty grasses
surged round her stranded body.

APRIL RISE

If ever I saw blessing in the air
   I see it now in this still early day
Where lemon-green the vaporous morning drips
   Wet sunlight on the powder of my eye.

Blown bubble-film of blue, the sky wraps round
   Weeds of warm light whose every root and rod
Splutters with soapy green, and all the world
   Sweats with the bead of summer in its bud.

If ever I heard blessing it is there
   Where birds in trees that shoals and shadows are
Splash with their hidden wings and drops of sound
   Break on my ears their crests of throbbing air.

Pure in the haze the emerald sun dilates,
   The lips of sparrows milk the mossy stones,
While white as water by the lake a girl
   Swims her green hand among the gathered swans.

Now, as the almond burns its smoking wick,
   Dropping small flames to light the candled grass;
Now, as my low blood scales its second chance,
   If ever world were blessèd, now it is.

DAY OF THESE DAYS

Such a morning it is when love
leans through geranium windows
and calls with a cockerel's tongue.

When red-haired girls scamper like roses
over the rain-green grass,
and the sun drips honey.

When hedgerows grow venerable,
berries dry black as blood,
and holes suck in their bees.

Such a morning it is when mice
run whispering from the church,
dragging dropped ears of harvest.

When the partridge draws back his spring
and shoots like a buzzing arrow
over grained and mahogany fields.

When no table is bare,
and no breast dry,
and the tramp feeds off ribs of rabbit.

Such a day it is when time
piles up the hills like pumpkins,
and the streams run golden.

When all men smell good,
and the cheeks of girls
are as baked bread to the mouth.

As bread and beanflowers
the touch of their lips,
and their white teeth sweeter than cucumbers.

THE LONG WAR

Less passionate the long war throws
its burning thorn about all men,
caught in one grief, we share one wound,
and cry one dialect of pain.

We have forgot who fired the house,
whose easy mischief spilt first blood,
under one raging roof we lie
the fault no longer understood.

But as our twisted arms embrace
the desert where our cities stood,
death's family likeness in each face
must show, at last, our brotherhood.

Christopher Logue

BLUES LAMENT

Tonight, I write sadly. Write,
For example: Little grasshopper,
Shelter from the midnight frost
In the scarecrow's sleeve, advising myself.

The night wind throbs in the sky.

Tonight, I write so wearily. Write,
For example: I wanted her,
And at times it was me she wanted. Write,
The rain we watched last fall

Has it fallen this year too?
She wanted me, and at times it was her
I wanted. Yet, it is gone, that want.
What's more, I do not care.

It is more terrible than my despair
Over losing her. The night, always vast,
Grows enormous without her, and
My comforter's tongue talking about her

Is a red fox barred by ivory, well,
Does it matter I loved too weak to keep her?
The night ignores such trivial disputes.
She is not here. That's all.

Far off someone is singing,
And if to bring her back I look,
And I run to the end of the road,
And I shout, shout her name,

My voice comes back the same, but weaker.

The night is the same night; it whitens
The same tree; casts similar shadows;
It is a dark, as long, as deep, and as endurable
As any other night. It is true: I do not want her.

But perhaps I want her . . .
Love's not as brief that I forget her,
So. Nevertheless, I shall forget her, and,
Alas, as if by accident.

A day will pass in which
I shall not think about her even once.
And this, the last line I shall write her.

THE SONG OF THE DEAD SOLDIER

For seven years at school I named
   Our kings, their wars—if these were won—
A boy trained simple as we come,
   I read of an island in the sun,
     Where the Queen of Love was born.

At seventeen the postman brought,
   Into the room—my place of birth—
Some correspondence from the Crown,
   Demanding that with guns I earn,
     The modern shilling I was worth.

Lucky for me that I could read,
   Lucky for me our captain said,
You'll see the world for free my son,
   You're posted to an island John,
     Where the Queen of Love was born.

So twenty weeks went by and by,
  My back was straightened out my eye
Dead true as any button shone,
  And nine white-bellied porpoise led,
  Our ship of shillings through the sun.

We landed with our drums and clad
  In war suits worth ten well-taxed pounds—
The costliest I ever had—
  Our foreign shoulders crossed the town,
  The Queen of Love our coloured flag.

And three by three through our curfew,
  Mother we marched like black and tan,
Singing to match our captain's cheers,
  Then I drank my eyes out of my head
  And wet Her shilling with my fears.

When morning came our captain bold
  Said the island shaped like an ass' skin
Must be kept calm, must be patrolled,
  For outposts are the heart and soul
  Of empire, love, and lawful rule.

I did not know to serve meant kill,
  And I did not see the captain fall,
As my life went out through a bullet hole,
  Mother, I said, your womb is done,
  Did they spend your English shilling well?

And then I saw a hag whose eyes
  Were big as medals and grey as lead,
I called my rifle but it was dead,
  Our captain roared but my ears went dud,
  The hag kissed warm, we met in blood.

  English shilling—Queen of Love.

GO TO THE WALL [1]

My father wanted to do right,
They said: Improve your mind.
He worked all day and read all night,
And now he's proud of being blind.
  Right gets you nowhere
  It goes on, that's all,
  Those who put their trust in right
  Go to the wall.

My brother cried: Give each his due,
The just must rule the strong.
They beat my brother black and blue
And swore that he was born a drum.
  The just change nothing
  They go on, that's all,
  Those who trust in justice
  Go to the wall.

My teacher said: The rich will fall
When men unite their claims.
They chained my teacher to the wall
And now he loves his chains.
  Men can change nothing
  They go on, that's all,
  Those who put their faith in men
  Go to the wall.

And now I hear that love provides
More calories than cream.
Better a slice of bacon, love,
Than a fat pig in a dream.
  Love gets you nowhere
  It goes on, that's all,
  Those who put their faith in love
  Go to the wall.

[1] from *The Lillywhite Boys*

Spike Milligan at the Hampstead Town Hall, 1962.
Photo Sydney Weaver

Spike Milligan

YE TORTURES

From a document found in the Archives of Bude Monastery during a squirting excavation. It shows a complete list of tortures, approved by the Ministry of Works in the year 1438, for failure to pay leg tithe, or sockage.

The prisoner will be:

    Bluned on ye Grunions
        and krelled on his Grotts
    Ye legges will be twergled
        and pulled thru' ye motts!

    His Nukes will be Fongled
        split thrice on yon Thulls
    Then laid on ye Quottle
        and hung by ye Bhuls!

    Twice thocked on the Phneffic,
        Yea broggled thrice twee.
    Ye moggs will be grendled
        and stretched six foot three!

    By now, if ye victim
        show not ye sorrow,
    Send him home. Tell him,
        "Come back to-morrow."

Laurie Lee reading at the Theatre Royal, Stratford East, 1964. In the background are Shake Keane (trumpet), Colin Barnes (drums), and Coleridge Goode (bass). *Photo Jane Gates*

RAIN

There are holes in the sky
   Where the rain gets in,
But they're ever so small
   That's why rain is thin.

PORRIDGE

Why is there no monument
   To Porridge in our land?
If it's good enough to eat
   It's good enough to stand!

On a plinth in London
   A statue we should see
Of Porridge made in Scotland
   Signed "Oatmeal, O.B.E."

Adrian Mitchell

BRIEFING

He may be fanatical, he may have a madness.
Either way, move carefully.
He must be surrounded, but he's contagious.

One of you will befriend his family.
One male and one female will love the subject
Until he loves you back. Gradually

Our team will abstract and collect
His mail, nail-clippings, garbage, friends, words, schemes,
Graphs of his fears, scars, sex and intellect.

Steam open his heart. Tap his dreams.
Learn him inside and inside out.
When he laughs, laugh. Scream when he screams.

He will scream, "Innocent!" He'll shout
Until his mouth is broken with stones.
We use stones. We take him out

To a valley full of stones.
He stands against a shed. He stands on stones
Naked. The initial stones

Shower the iron shed. Those stones
Outline the subject. When he cries for stones
The clanging ceases. Then we give him stones,

Filling his universe with stones.
Stones—his atoms turn to stones
And he becomes a stone buried in stones.

A final tip. Then you may go.
Note the half-hearted stoners and watch how
Your own arm throws. And watch how I throw.

NOSTALGIA—NOW THREEPENCE OFF

Where are they now, the heroes of furry-paged books and comics brighter than life which packed my inklined desk in days when BOP meant Boys' Own Paper, where are they anyway?

Where is Percy F. Westerman? Where are H. L. Gee and Arthur Mee? Where is Edgar Rice (The Warlord of Mars), Burroughs, the Bumper Fun Book and the Wag's Handbook? Where is the Wonder Book of Reptiles? Where the hell is The Boy's Book of Bacteriological Warfare?

Where are the Beacon Readers? Did Ro-ver, that tireless hound, devour his mon-o-syll-ab-ic-all-y correct family? Did Little Black Sambo and Epaminondas shout for Black Power?

Did Peter Rabbit get his when myxomatosis came round the second time, did the Flopsy Bunnies stiffen to a standstill, grow bug-eyed, fly-covered and then disintegrate?

Where is G. A. Henty and his historical lads—Wolfgang the Hittite, Armpit the Young Viking, Cyril who lived in Sodom? Where are their uncorrupted bodies and Empire-building brains, England needs them, the *Sunday Times* says so.

There is news from Strewelpeter mob. Johnny-Head-In-Air spends his days reporting flying saucers, the telephone receiver never cools from the heat of his hand. Little Harriet, who played with matches, still burns, but not with fire. The Scissor-man is everywhere.

Babar the Elephant turned the jungle into a garden city. But things went wrong. John and Susan, Titty and Roger, became unaccountably afraid of water, sold their dinghies, all married each other, live in a bombed-out cinema on surgical spirits and weeds of all kinds.

Snow White was in the *News of the World*—Virgin Lived With Seven Midgets, Court Told. And in the psychiatric ward an old woman dribbles as she mumbles about a family of human bears, they ate porridge, yes Miss Goldilocks of course they did.

Hans Brinker vainly whirled his silver skates round his head as the jackboots of Emil and the Detectives invaded his Resistance Cellar.

Some failed. Desperate Dan and Meddlesome Matty and Strang the Terrible and Korky the Cat killed themselves with free gifts in a back room at the Peter Pan Club because they were impotent, like us. Their audience, the senile Chums of Red Circle School, still wearing for reasons of loyalty and lust the tatters of their uniforms, voted that exhibition a super wheeze.

Some succeeded. Tom Sawyer's heart has cooled, his ingenuity flowers at Cape Canaveral.

But they are all trodden on, the old familiar faces, so at the rising of the sun and the going down of the ditto I remember I remember the house where I was taught to play up play up and play the game though nobody told me what the game was, but we know now, don't we, we know what the game is, but lives of great men all remind us we can make our lives sublime and departing leave behind us arseprints on the sands of time, but the tide's come up, the castles are washed down, where are they now, where are they, where are the deep shelters? There are no deep shelters. Biggles may drop it, Worrals of the Wraaf may press the button. So, Billy and Bessie Bunter, prepare for the last and cosmic Yarooh and throw away the Man-Tan. The sky will soon be full of suns.

FIFTEEN MILLION PLASTIC BAGS

I was walking in a government warehouse
Where the daylight never goes.
I saw fifteen million plastic bags
Hanging in a thousand rows.

Five million bags were six feet long
Five million bags were five foot five
Five million were stamped with Mickey Mouse
And they came in a smaller size.

Were they for guns or uniforms
Or a dirty kind of party game?
Then I saw each bag had a number
And every bag bore a name.

And five million bags were six feet long
Five million were five foot five
Five million were stamped with Mickey Mouse
And they came in a smaller size

So I've taken my bag from the hanger
And I've pulled it over my head
And I'll wait for the priest to zip it
So the radiation won't spread

Now five million bags are six feet long
Five million are five foot five
Five million are stamped with Mickey Mouse
And they come in a smaller size.

Dom Moraes

THE GARDEN

I wake and find myself in love:
And this one time I do not doubt.
I only fear, and wander out
To hold long parley with a dove.

The innocent and the guilty, met
Here in the garden, feel no fear.
But I'm afraid of you, my dear.
There was a reason: I forget.

And I by shyness am undone
And can't go out for fear I meet
My poems dancing down the street
Telling your name to everyone.

The lichen peels along the wall.
My conversation bores the dove.
He knows it all: that I'm in love
And you care much and not at all.

I shall stay here and keep my word.
Glumly I wait to marry dust.
It grieves me only that I must
Speak not to you, but to a bird.

JOHN NOBODY

I slam the door. Outside I find the day
Unkempt and soused. My muddy shoes seek those
Tenants of me who lately moved away.
It irks me now, the other homes they chose.

It irks me now, so many lying so stiff,
Locked into rock, or smudged with mud like paint.
When graveyard shifts of wind diffuse the whiff
It would try the nostrils of any saint.

It irks me too that someone else's hands
Touch you I love and hardly ever meet.
Rest your tired mind, for I make no demands.
Do not so much as see me in the street.

A better meeting we may have one day
When with long years and whisky I forget.
Years, but I am already on the way,
Though I decline to walk, my shoes are wet.

Buses, however, bore me—the delay!
Endless!—and you can only smoke upstairs.
The underground for me, its walls display
Advertisements with girls in brassieres.

So, an attentive eye fixed on the knees
Of the young woman opposite, I go
West the best way I can, a cindery breeze
About my ears, thunder and sparks below,

West to my rendezvous, to the plush bar
Where a flushed rose, all petalled lips and scent,
Ample of breast, your sexual avatar,
Billows her new coat like a little tent.

Traffic of childhood dreams roars through my head.
A woman dancing on a windy shore,
Lifting her white arms, beckoned me to bed.
Was it then, or today, I slammed the door,

Refuge behind me, and a labyrinth
Opening under me, wet, dark and dense?
It was the winter of my seventeenth
Year when I lost what some call innocence.

Lightly that night the snow fell on Belgrade
And that time Djilas was in prison there.
The students pranced at every barricade
With rolling eyes like ponies, restless hair.

But riots in the square, shots after dark,
Scarcely disturbed her fringed eyes where she lay,
Who floated on our bed, her quilted ark,
Into a dream of landfall in the day.

Her lashes hid two rinsed bits of the sky.
Aged twelve, the German troops had noticed her.
A patient queue of sergeants formed nearby
While four men held her for the officer.

But my new playmate thinks she might enjoy
Being raped (no man has needed to before):
Venturing which, she giggles and looks coy,
Then browses, tranquil as some herbivore

Above the leaves and fruit left in her drink.
I can't afford another, but repine
Little, and leave her here to sit and think,
And what she thinks is no concern of mine.

From Iceland now a slowly kicking wind
Trails its long legs across the northern sea,
Collapses down the Strand, and in my mind
Sets constipated windmills spinning free.

They churn!—loose images fall at my heel.
No use to me, and so I leave them there.
Last August in the Valley of Jezreel,
Homesick, I dreamt about Trafalgar Square.

But in the Square today, I dream of hawks,
Of doelike girls, the sun, endless delay,
Bullocks and Buicks, statesmen like great auks,
And I grow homesick for an Indian day.

But there, last year, a moral issue rose.
I grabbed my pen and galloped to attack.
My Rosinante trod on someone's toes.
A Government frowned, and now I can't go back.

The helpful rain repeats the news, meanwhile
Scrubbing bird relics off Lord Nelson's hat
And I go praying down my crooked mile
Like her in Belgrade, for an Ararat.

The patchwork ark that buoyed me for a year,
You at the tiller, when you left it, sank.
I know you had to think of your career.
I knew it all the while, therefore I drank.

Yet I thought, as the loving tide nosed higher
Around my neck, surely in straits like these
Verse based on you would prise me from the mire.
I was misled by old Archimedes.

No hint of light filters to the morass
Where I submerge, this afternoon, and hide.
I observe people darkly through a glass.
A spewing slot machine stands by my side.

I milk smoke from my cigarette, and puff
Inexpert rings at it, and startled, see
Through a blurred haze of whisky, smoke and love,
My friends' annealing faces rise to me.

They fade: some cubic inches of used air
Tease my imagination: I still wait,
Imprisoned in the framework of my chair
For angels: but today they hibernate.

So I must smile at mirrors when I can
For company, though without much goodwill.
The newspaper I borrow from a man
Tells me in London it is raining still,

Which means another drink would do no harm.
So to the bar for one more double Scotch.
The barman looks at me in slight alarm
And looks from me, brows lifted, at his watch.

My income and my debts remain the same.
Still, I can feed my typewriter each day.
My agents tells me that I have a name.
An audience waits, he says, for what I say,

My audience!—kempt, virtuous, and strange:
Those delicate, flushed girls with eyes like stars,
So lately come from college, long to change
The creature they observe in dingy bars.

The creature they observe sways where it stands,
Lifting uncertain arms as if to bless.
Even so great a gesture of the hands
Can hardly hold so vast an emptiness.

RENDEZVOUS[1]

(For Nathan Altermann)

Altermann, sipping wine, reads with a look
Of infinite patience and slight suffering.
When I approach him, he puts down his book,

Waves to the chair beside him like a king,
Then claps his hands, and an awed waiter fetches
Bread, kosher sausage, cake, a chicken's wing,

More wine, some English cigarettes, and matches.
"Eat, eat," Altermann says, "this is good food."
Through the awning over us the sunlight catches

His aquiline sad head, till it seems hewed
From tombstone marble. I accept some bread.
I've lunched already, but would not seem rude.

When I refuse more, he feeds me instead,
Heaping my plate, clapping for wine, his eyes
—Expressionless inside the marble head—

Appearing not to notice how the flies
Form a black, sticky icing on the cake.
Thinking of my health now, I visualise

The Aryan snow floating, flake upon flake,
Over the ghetto wall where only fleas
Fed well, and they and hunger kept awake

Under sharp stars, those waiting for release.
Birds had their nests, but Jews nowhere to hide
When visited by vans and black police.

[1] *Part 1 of a sequence of "Two poems from Israel"*

The shekinah rose where a people died,
A pillar of flame by night, of smoke by day.
From Europe then the starved and terrified

Flew. Now their mourner sits in this café,
Telling me how to scan a Hebrew line.
Though my attention has moved far away

His features stay marble and aquiline.
But the eternal gesture of his race
Flowing through the hands that offer bread and wine

Reveals the deep love sealed in the still face.

SNOW ON A MOUNTAIN

That dream, her eyes like rocks studded the high
Mountain of her body that I was to climb.
   One moment past my hands had swum
   The chanting streams of her thighs:
Then I was lost, breathless among the pines.

Alone, alone with the nervous noise of water,
Climbing, I hoped to emerge on a path, but I knew
   When the spurred trees were past
   I should go on no farther
But fall there, dazzled by the miles of snow.

My dream was broken by the knock of day.
Yet, within my mind, these pictures linger:
   I touched her with my clumsy words of love
   And sense snow in her eye,
Mists, and the winds that warn, Stranger, O stranger!

Peter Porter

METAMORPHOSIS

This new Daks suit, greeny-brown,
Oyster coloured buttons, single vent, tapered
Trousers, no waistcoat, hairy tweed—my own:
A suit to show responsibility, to show
Return to life—easily got for two pounds down
Paid off in six months—the first stage in the change.
I am only the image I can force upon the town.

The town will have me: I stalk in glass,
A thin reflection in the windows, best
In jewellers' velvet background—I don't pass,
I stop, elect to look at wedding rings—
My figure filled with clothes, my putty mask,
A face fragrant with arrogance, stuffed
With recognition—I am myself at last.

I wait in the pub with my Worthington.
Then you come in—how many days did love have,
How can they be catalogued again?
We talk of how we miss each other—I tell
Some truth—you, cruel stories built of men:
"It wasn't good at first but he's improving."
More talk about his car, his drinks, his friends.

I look to the wild mirror at the bar—
A beautiful girl smiles beside me—she's real
And her regret is real. If only I had a car,
If only—my stately self cringes, renders down:
As in a werewolf film I'm horrible, far
Below the collar—my fingers crack, my tyrant suit
Chokes me as it hugs me in its fire.

ANNOTATIONS OF AUSCHWITZ

I

When the burnt flesh is finally at rest,
The fires in the asylum grates will come up
And wicks turn down to darkness in the madman's eyes.

II

My suit is hairy, my carpet smells of death,
My toothbrush handle grows a cuticle.
I have six million foulnesses of breath.
Am I mad? The doctor holds my testicles
While the room fills with the zyklon B I cough.

III

On Piccadilly underground I fall asleep—
I shuffle with the naked to the steel door,
Now I am only ten from the front—I wake up—
We are past Gloucester Rd, I am not a Jew,
But scratches web the ceiling of the train.

IV

Around staring buildings the pale flowers grow:
The frenetic butterfly, the bee made free by work,
Rouse and rape the pollen pads, the nectar stoops.
The rusting railway ends here. The blind end in Europe's gut.
Touch one piece of unstrung barbed wire—
Let it taste blood: let one man scream in pain,
Death's Botanical Gardens can flower again.

V

A man eating his dressing in the hospital
Is lied to by his stomach. It's final feast to him
Of beef, blood pudding and black bread.
The orderly can't bear to see this mimic face
With its prim accusing picture after death.
On the stiff square a thousand bodies
Dig up useless ground—he hates them all,
These lives ignoble as ungoverned glands.
They fatten in statistics everywhere
And with their sick, unkillable fear of death
They crowd out peace from executioners' sleep.

VI

Forty thousand bald men drowning in a stream—
The like of light on all those bobbing skulls
Has never been seen before. Such death, says the painter,
Is worthwhile—it makes a colour never known.
It makes a sight that's unimagined, says the poet.
It's nothing to do with me, says the man who hates
The poet and the painter. Six million deaths can hardly
Occur at once. What do they make? Perhaps
An idiot's normalcy. I need never feel afraid
When I salt the puny snail—cruelty's grown up
And waits for time and men to bring into its hands
The snail's adagio and all the taunting life
Which has not cared about or guessed its tortured scope.

VII

London is full of chickens on electric spits,
    Cooking in windows where the public pass.
This, say the chickens, is their Auschwitz,
    And all poultry eaters are psychopaths.

Dom Moraes, photographed in 1968

JOHN MARSTON ADVISES ANGER

All the boys are howling to take the girls to bed.
Our betters say it's a seedy world. The critics say
Think of them as an Elizabethan Chelsea set.
Then they've never listened to our lot—no talk
Could be less like—but the bodies are the same:
Those jeans and bums and sweaters of the King's Road
Would fit Marston's stage. What's in a name,
If Cheapside and the Marshalsea mean Eng. Lit.
And the Fantasie, Sa Tortuga, Grisbi, Bongi-Bo
Mean life? A cliché? What hurts dies on paper,
Fades to classic pain. Love goes as the M.G. goes.
The colonel's daughter in black stockings, hair
Like sash cords, face iced white, studies art,
Goes home once a month. She won't marry the men
She sleeps with, she'll revert to type—it's part
Of the side-show: Mummy and Daddy in the wings,
The bongos fading on the road to Haslemere
Where the inheritors are inheriting still.
Marston's Malheureux found his whore too dear;
Today some Jazz Club girl on the social make
Would put him through his paces, the aphrodisiac cruel.
His friends would be the smoothies of our Elizabethan age—
The Rally Men, Grantchester Breakfast Men, Public School
Personal Assistants and the fragrant P.R.Os.,
Cavalry-twilled tame publishers praising Logue,
Classics Honours Men promoting Jazzetry,
Market Researchers married into Vogue.
It's a Condé Nast world and so Marston's was.
His had a real gibbet—our death's out of sight.
The same thin richness of these worlds remains—
The flesh-packed jeans, the car-stung appetite
Volley on his stage, the cage of discontent.

Adrian Mitchell at the Centre 42 Festival, Leicester, 1962.
Photo John Hopkins

MADE IN HEAVEN

From Heals and Harrods come her lovely bridegrooms
(One cheque alone furnished two bedrooms),

From a pantechnicon in the dog-paraded street
Under the orange plane leaves, on workmen's feet

Crunching over Autumn, the fruits of marriage brought
Craftsman-felt wood, Swedish dressers, a court

Stool tastefully imitated and the wide bed—
(the girl who married money kept her maiden head).

As things were ticked off the Harrods list, there grew
A middle-class maze to pick your way through—

The labour-saving kitchen to match the labour-saving thing
She'd fitted before marriage (O Love, with this ring

I thee wed)—lastly the stereophonic radiogram
And her Aunt's sly letter promising a pram.

Settled in now, the Italian honeymoon over,
As the relatives said, she was living in clover.

The discontented drinking of a few weeks stopped,
She woke up one morning to her husband's alarm-clock,

Saw the shining faces of the wedding gifts from the bed,
Foresaw the cosy routine of the massive years ahead.

As she watched her husband knot his tie for the city,
She thought: I wanted to be a dancer once—it's a pity.

I've done none of the things I thought I wanted to,
Found nothing more exacting than my own looks, got through

Half a dozen lovers whose faces I can't quite remember
(I can still start the Rose Adagio, one foot on the fender)

But at least I'm safe from everything but cancer—
The apotheosis of the young wife and mediocre dancer.

YOUR ATTENTION PLEASE

The Polar DEW has just warned that
A nuclear rocket strike of
At least one thousand megatons
Has been launched by the enemy
Directly at our major cities.
This announcement will take
Two and a quarter minutes to make,
You therefore have a further
Eight and a quarter minutes
To comply with the shelter
Requirements published in the Civil
Defence Code—section Atomic Attack.
A specially shortened Mass
Will be broadcast at the end
Of this announcement—
Protestant and Jewish services
Will begin simultaneously—
Select your wavelength immediately
According to instructions
In the Defence Code. Do not
Take well-loved pets (including birds)
Into your shelter—they will consume
Fresh air. Leave the old and bed-
ridden, you can do nothing for them.
Remember to press the sealing
Switch when everyone is in
The shelter. Set the radiation

Aerial, turn on the geiger barometer.
Turn off your Television now.
Turn off your radio immediately
The Services end. At the same time
Secure explosion plugs in the ears
Of each member of your family. Take
Down your plasma flasks. Give your children
The pills marked one and two
In the C.D. green container, then put
Them to bed. Do not break
The inside airlock seals until
The radiation All Clear shows
(Watch for the cuckoo in your
perspex panel), or your District
Touring Doctor rings your bell.
If before this, your air becomes
Exhausted or if any of your family
Is critically injured, adminster
The capsules marked "Valley Forge"
(Red pocket in No. 1 Survival Kit)
For painless death. (Catholics
Will have been instructed by their priests
What to do in this eventuality.)
This announcement is ending. Our President
Has already given orders for
Massive retaliation—it will be
Decisive. Some of us may die.
Remember, statistically
It is not likely to be you.
All flags are flying fully dressed
On Government buildings—the sun is shining.
Death is the least we have to fear.
We are all in the hands of God,
Whatever happens happens by His Will.
Now go quickly to your shelters.

Jeremy Robson

WAKING

Waking, you said you saw your house,
the Nile snaking into mist,
Mohammed the one-eyed cook.
Somehow, you said, there were children,
running . . .

And I have watched you waking,
breaking from an Orient
half-hinted at in gestures, frowns,
a craze for things with spice,
pepper, pomegranate, pimento, rice,
love of the desert, rock, the open sky.

And in you, grave refugee,
I catch an ancient plight:
not crammed in trucks
not stoned on sight
hounded by Inquisition
or crusading zeal,
but turned
without word without sound
from shore to sea: Suez, '56—
a Cairo-born French-speaking
Spanish Jewess on the wing.

It was wonderful, marvellous, you say
the late sun thumbing the Nile
the children running . . .
And away you go into dream:
the new London day dismissed
the four safe walls,
the friend that guards, regards you,

comes so close, retreats,
hearing a voice troubled in sleep
calling a new name, in a strange tongue,
distant and complete.

JUST CALL

You only have to speak:
I must respond,
move from my chair
to see to this or that,
answer you, refrain,
nod, shrug, explain.

The phone, at any hour:
I have to jump from sleep
to check that this one's well
that one free,
to say when we can come
when we cannot.

Raised voices on the train:
I'm soon drawn in,
lured on to speculate
how she would rate,
if he'll hold down his job, his girl,
if she, if he, if she . . .

Transistors blaze: forced to overhear.
Headlines stare: compelled to read.
Faces, voices, devils in my dreams: ensnared.
Call my name, sing your psalms, make your war,
speak your speech, Save my Soul. . . .
Break down my door: I wait.

TRAVELLING

The Adriatic. Night. Lights
in waves of yellows, blues, and greens
ignite the trees: bats swerve between.
A random line recurs—
"Green the shadows in your hair."
The music slurs.
The wine is sugar-sweet.
Campari grates.

*

Urbino: Raphael's house,
alongside steep steps, guttered.
The mind, assaulted, notes
notes first the lounge,
bedroom, study of the Master,
the lounge especially—
large, white, the place for nights
for reverie, where light decants.
Nearby, encased, five letters
from an English lord
who restored the place in '73
making it (to quote) accessible
to His public: a fresco
by an erstwhile host ignores.
The host has fled.

Outside, half a mile away,
the towered palace of Frederic the one-eyed
Urbino's patron Duke who gave the place its page
(at Pesaro Rossini's house was grave).
Two paintings stay like lovers on the mind:
della Francesca's *Flagellation of Christ*,
Uccello's *Profanation of the Host*.

*

Travelling: the car exploring
mountain bends blindly.
The brakes are dicey,
and my hands tense.
Three hours and the journey's won.
On either side the Arno,
quicksilver in the sun.
Two ghost-like words accost
   Americani Assassini!
The accelerator's down.
Soon Florence,
a room to kill the light.
The shadows on your lips are brown.

*

And Florence: its famed Cathedral, marble
baptistry, chequered green on white.
Giotto's Campanile on the right.
Your arms are bare.
A pious doorman moves
to block our way.
A sharp exchange, and then we step inside,
go "naked before the Lord".
Angry, I note the arms of Christ
in Michelangelo's *Pietà*, bare.
The church is dark.
Your stomach pains
and migraine cramps my eyes.
We edge towards the day.

The shadows on Christ's arms were grey.

BACK

Back down that street
avoiding the cracks in paving stones
vaulting high walls
ringing door bells
running
summoning hidden heroes
from behind trees, from behind hills,
D'Artagnan, Cassidy. . . .

Back on that station
counting ten-second ultimatums
to expected trains:
not here in ten seconds
I'll jump, I'll scream.
Ten, nine, eight. . . .

That high-domed room again
caught by the cracked prayers
of the shawled, swaying men
   We pledge this
   Deliver us from that
   Bring us peace Bring us rain
   Hasten our Return

Back, smug conqueror, to that school,
that nightmare, jam-jar world,
now fictionalised, removed.
Same odours, sickening smells,
same names, desks, corridors,
same fears and rituals
   Let us pray
   Let us recall those colleagues
   Who gave their young lives

Same men, same masters, searching,
reaching back: "Your name?"
"Were you here in. . . ."
Ten years. Now back, unknown,
unrecognised abstraction.
Let us recall. . . .

Tight-packed, queuing ghosts,
ten, nine, eight,
dust to dust,
gone, returned, pressing the nerves,
waiting the counting, the reckoning,
the long-knived, jackboot nights.

SONG FOR A SEASON

Under a sun, under a moon
walk fast, walk slow,
and still the voices come
and still the voices go.

Rivers to the ocean
lovers to the war,
and still the waters freeze
and still the bombers soar.

Once I chased a shadow
once I stalked a ghost,
caught the voices lying
found I was their host.

And still the voices drum
and still the voices grow,
soldiers to the killing
driftwood to the flow.

Vernon Scannell

TAKEN IN ADULTERY

Shadowed by shades and spied upon by glass
Their search for privacy conducts them here,
With an irony that neither notices,
To a public house; the wrong time of the year
For outdoor games; where, over gin and tonic,
Best bitter and potato crisps, they talk
Without much zest, almost laconic,
Flipping an occasional remark.
Would you guess that they were lovers, this dull pair?
The answer, I suppose, is yes, you would.
Despite her spectacles and faded hair
And his worn look of being someone's Dad
You know that they are having an affair
And neither finds it doing them much good.
Presumably, in one another's eyes,
They must look different from what we see,
Desirable in some way, otherwise
They'd hardly choose to come here, furtively,
And mutter their bleak needs above the mess
Of fag-ends, crumpled cellophane and crumbs,
Their love-feast's litter. Though they might profess
To find great joy together, all that comes
Across to us is tiredness, melancholy.
When they are silent each seems listening;
There must be many voices in the air:
Reproaches, accusations, suffering
That no amount of passion keeps elsewhere.
Imperatives that brought them to this room,
Stiff from the car's back seat, lose urgency;
They start to wonder who's betraying whom,
How it will end, and how did it begin—
The woman taken in adultery
And the man who feels he, too, was taken in.

AN OLD LAMENT RENEWED

The soil is savoury with their bones' lost marrow;
   Down among dark roots their polished knuckles lie,
And no one could tell one peeled head from another;
   Earth packs each crater that once gleamed with eye.

Colonel and batman, emperor and assassin,
   Democratised by silence and corruption,
Defy identification with identical grin:
   The joke is long, will brook no interruption.

At night the imagination walks like a ghoul
   Among the stone lozenges and counterpanes of turf
Tumescent under cypresses; the long, rueful call
   Of the owl soars high and then wheels back to earth.

And brooding over the enormous dormitory
   The mind grows shrill at those nothings in lead rooms
Who were beautiful once or dull and ordinary,
   But loved, all loved, all called to sheltering arms.

Many I grieve with a grave, deep love
   Who are deep in the grave, whose faces I never saw:
Poets who died of alcohol, bullets, or birthdays
   Doss in the damp house, forbidden now to snore.

And in a French orchard lies whatever is left
   Of my friend, Gordon Rennie, whose courage would toughen
The muscle of resolution; he laughed
   At death's serious face, but once too often.

On summer evenings when the religious sun stains
   The gloom in the bar and the glasses surrender demurely
I think of Donovan whose surrender was unconditional,
   That great thirst swallowed entirely.

And often some small thing will summon the memory
   Of my small son, Benjamin. A smile is his sweet ghost.
But behind, in the dark, the white twigs of his bones
   Form a pattern of guilt and waste.

I am in mourning for the dull, the heroic and the mad;
   In the haunted nursery the child lies dead.
I mourn the hangman and his bulging complement;
   I mourn the cadaver in the egg.

The one-eyed rider aims, shoots death into the womb;
   Blood on the sheet of snow, the maiden dead.
The dagger has a double blade and meaning,
   So has the double bed.

Imagination swaggers in the sensual sun
   But night will find it at the usual mossy gate;
The whisper from the mouldering darkness comes:
   "I am the one you love and fear and hate."

I know my grieving is made thick by terror;
   The bones of those I loved aren't fleshed by sorrow.
I mourn the deaths I've died and go on dying;
   I fear the long, implacable tomorrow.

THE MEN WHO WEAR MY CLOTHES

Sleepless I lay last night and watched the slow
   Procession of the men who wear my clothes:
First, the grey man with bloodshot eyes and sly
   Gestures miming what he loves and loathes.

Next came the cheery knocker-back of pints,
   The beery joker, never far from tears
Whose loud and public vanity acquaints
   The careful watcher with his private fears.

And then I saw the neat-mouthed gentle man
   Defer politely, listen to the lies,
Smile at the tedious talk and gaze upon
   The little mirrors in the speaker's eyes.

The men who wear my clothes walked past my bed
   And all of them looked tired and rather old;
I felt a chip of ice melt in my blood.
   Naked I lay last night and very cold.

NO SENSE OF DIRECTION

I have always admired
Those who are sure
Which turning to take,
Who need no guide
Even in war
When thunders shake
The torn terrain,
When battalions of shrill
Stars all desert

And the derelict moon
Goes over the hill:
Eyes chained by the night
They find their way back
As if it were daylight.
Then, on peaceful walks
Over strange wooded ground
They will find the right track,
Know which of the forks
Will lead to the inn
I would never have found;
For I lack their gift,
Possess almost no
Sense of direction.
And yet I owe
A debt to this lack,
A debt so vast
No reparation
Can ever be made,
For it led me away
From the road I sought
Which would carry me to—
I mistakenly thought—
My true destination:
It made me stray
To this lucky path
That ran like a fuse
And brought me to you
And love's bright, soundless
Detonation.

I'M COVERED NOW

"What would happen to your lady wife
And little ones—you've four I think you said—
Little ones I mean, not wives, ha-ha—
What would happen to them if . . ." And here
He cleared his throat of any reticence.
". . . if something happened to you? We've got to face
These things, must be realistic, don't you think?
Now, we have various schemes to give you cover
And, taking in account your age and means,
This policy would seem to be the one . . ."

The words uncoiled, effortless but urgent,
Assured, yet coming just a bit too fast,
A little breathless, despite the ease of manner,
An athlete drawing near the tape's last gasp
Yet trying hard to seem still vigorous there.
But no, this metaphor has too much muscle;
His was an indoor art and every phrase
Was handled with a trained seducer's care.
I took the words to heart, or, if not heart,
Some region underneath intelligence,
The area where the hot romantic aria
And certain kinds of poetry are received.
And this Giovanni of the fast buck knew
My humming brain was pleasurably numb;
My limbs were weakening; he would soon achieve
The now sequestered ends for which he'd come.

At last I nodded, glazed, and said I'd sign,
But he showed little proper satisfaction.
He sighed and sounded almost disappointed,
And I remembered hearing someone say
No Juan really likes an easy lay.

Upper: Jeremy Robson at Hereford College, 1968. *Photo Richard Lake*
Lower: Stevie Smith at the Theatre Royal, Stratford East, 1965.
Photo Ken Coton

But I'll say this: he covered up quite quickly
And seemed almost as ardent as before
When he pressed my hand and said that he was happy
And hoped that I was, too.
                           And then the door
Was closed behind him as our deal was closed.
If something happened I was covered now.
Odd that I felt so chilly, so exposed.

Vernon Scannell (reading) and John Smith at the Purcell Room, 1967.
Photo Ilana Steinitz

Jon Silkin

THE CUNNING OF AN AGE

   The fox sat under the hill.
And all around him the day was springing the earth
Curved away in a style he knew to be home;
The year grew around him like a love, the birds
Cried down the wind

   And the air hummed with growing.
He smelt the humble plants at the foot of the hill.
The grass was bleeding like love and the insects stirred
In the air at ease with themselves. The black wind streamed
Over the top of the hill.

   Only here had he made a home.
The ways of the world had stopped short of this bulge
On the surface of things because . . . because it had other
Things to do. And the fox sat under the hill
And all lay still.

   Yet as he sat there wondering
How rivers came to be especially
His one at the edge of the world his world, a spot
Of red spat up at his eyes, no more, and was gone
In a twist of vision. No more than that

   To the fox who sat under the hill.
The air was the same the year went round just the same
The insects turned around in their aimless journeys.
But just that red at the foot of the hill below
The stream had changed things.

Jon Silkin 115

   Had changed his home
To a starting place, and below came the horn's winding
Warning halloo and up he was and smartly
Away as the red shot up to his horizon
And his mind's horizon.

   And he was away.
No listening or waiting for the will and lust
Of the world but to live and lick his life
From the corners of a world that would hold him easily
Peacefully was his will,

   Under a hill of maiden-hair
And grass as green as blood and summer-time
To sweat in his fur and his ways. He was off to save
His life. The hounds were baying the other side
Of the hill. And

   He thought as he ran with his name
of the names he'd been told and the games he'd been called, but
    the horn
Whirled round in his head and the hounds fell on
In the leaps that distance and time pulls on one, the tricks
The mind pulls on one.

   And the wind changed his name
To FOLLOWED from Fox-on-the-hill
And the wind followed, curling his brush. And the hounds
    followed too,
Like dreams like death on the hill like birds like grass
Like anything but not

Like fox he was
Or fox he knew and the horn curled round in his head
Slipping over the hill and into his head. But here
He swerved and hid. And the hounds went hurling past
With blood before

Their eyes, and the men and the world
With blood over their hands and a curse on their whips
And a horse on their world and a horn on their minds
Went for a day
Over and down the hill.

SACRED

I have talked with respectable women
Many of whom declare
The several fingered dew
Laid on a man's parts is love.
More naked is love; some say
Pure, like a glacier:
Yet congruous as despair,
Or rather something
Meaner than vanity.
For one with coarse-grained hand
Ties her sharp ribbon to
Her hair while, binding him,
Yells, "love O love", though she
Takes with an ancient care
Ever to give what is
Part of security.

There are others too, numerous
As sand-grain who sweat for
Not ambition but bread,
Having all but the seminal part
Of coarse men and cold men
Unenamoured of love
And love's perplexities.

So here, besides the cash
I give you a steel necklace
To be worn near the flesh
As conduit, a flow of
Hand-made steel ornamentation:

So many lesser than you
So many professing love
Less capable of that
And who are bought, and know it
May not pretend to passion.
Incapable of passion
They move with a rigid glare
Beneath their horror.

Nothing of tenderness
Will ever touch in them
For child or animal
Much generosity.

You to whom too much
Is given, but no love—
It is so much you give me
The tenderness you give now
Though that is bought from you,
That having little to offer
This much of you is more
Than others surrendering;
More than respectable women
More than such practised thieves.

MOSS

"Patents" will burn it out; it would lie there
Turning white. It shelters on the soil; quilts it.
So persons lie over it; but look closely:
The thick, short green threads quiver like an animal
As a fungoid quivers between that and vegetable:
A mushroom's flesh with the texture and consistency of a kidney.

Moss is soft as a pouch.
There are too many shoots though, boxed compacted,
Yet nestling together,
Softly luminous.
They squirm minutely. The less compact kind
Has struggling white flowers; closed,
Like a minute bell's clapper;
So minute that opened then, its stretch seems wide.
The first grows in damper places.
With what does it propagate?
Quiet, of course, it adheres to
The cracks of waste-pipes, velvets,
Velours them; an enriching
Unnatural ruff swathing the urban "manifestation":
The urban nature is basemented, semi-dark;
It musts, it is alone.

Here moss cools; it has no children;
It amplifies itself.
Could that over-knit fiction of stubbed threads reproduce
Defined creatures?
It hovers tentatively between one life and another,
Being the closed-road of plants,
Its mule; spreads only its kind—
A soft stone. It is not mad.

ASTRINGENCIES
(1 THE COLDNESS)

Where the printing-works buttress a church
And the northern river like moss
Robes herself slowly through
The cold township of York,
More slowly than usual
For a cold, northern river,
You see the citizens
Indulging stately pleasures,
Like swans. But they seem cold.
Why have they been so punished;
In what do their sins consist now?
An assertion persistent
As a gross tumour, and the sense
Of such growth haunting
The flesh of York
Is that there has been
No synagogue since eleven ninety
When eight hundred Jews
Took each other's lives
To escape christian death
By christian hand; and the last
Took his own. The event
Has the frigid persistence of a growth
In the flesh. It is a fact
No other fact can be added to
Save that it was Easter, the time
When the dead christian God
Rose again. It is in this,
Perhaps, they are haunted; for the cold
Blood of victims is colder,
More staining, more corrosive

On the soul, than the blood of martyrs.
What consciousness is there of the cold
Heart, with its spaces?
For nothing penetrates
More than admitted absence.
The heart in warmth, even, cannot
Close its gaps. Absence of Jews
Through hatred, or indifference,
A gap they slip through, a conscience
That corrodes more deeply since it is
Forgotten—this deadens York.
Where are the stone-masons, the builders
Skilled in glass, strong first in wood;
Taut, flaxen plumbers with lengths of pipe,
Steel rules coiled in their palms;
The printers; canopy-makers—
Makers in the institution of marriage?
Their absence is endless, a socket
Where the jaw is protected neither
Through its tolerance for tooth,
Nor for blood. Either there is pain or no pain.
If they could feel; were there one
Among them with this kind
Of sensitivity that
Could touch the dignity,
Masonry of the cold
Northern face that falls
As you touch it, there might
Be some moving to
A northern expurgation.
All Europe is touched
With some of frigid York,
As York is now by Europe.

John Smith

DEATH AT THE OPERA

Is this what death is like? I sit
Dressed elegantly in black and white, in an expensive seat,
Watching Violetta expire in Covent Garden.
How beautiful she is! As her voice lures me toward her death
The strings of the orchestra moisten my eyes with tears,
Though the tenor is too loud. Is this what death is like?
No one moves. Violetta coughs; stumbles toward the bed.
Twenty miles away in the country my father is dying.
Violetta catches at her throat. Let me repeat: My father
Is dying in a semi-detached house on a main road
Twenty miles off in the country. The skull is visible.

I do not want it to end. How exquisitely moving is death,
The approach to it. The lovers sob. Soon they will be wrenched apart.
How romantic it all is. Her hand is a white moth
Fluttering against the coverlet of the bed. The bones
Of my father's hands poke through his dry skin.
His eyes look into a vacancy of space. He spits into a cup.
In a few moments now Violetta will give up the ghost;
The doctor, the maid, the tenor who does not love her, will sob.
Almost, our hearts will stop beating. How refreshed we have been.
My father's clothes, too large for his shrunken frame,
Make him look like a parcel. Ah! The plush curtains are opening.

The applause! The applause! It drowns out the ugly noise
Of my father's choking and spitting. The bright lights
Glitter far more than the 100 Watt bulb at home.
Dear Violetta! How she enjoys the flowers, like wreaths,

Showered for her own death. She gathers them to her.
We have avoided the coffin. I think that my father
Would like a box of good plain beech, being a man
From Buckinghamshire, a man of the country, a man of the soil.
I have seen my father, who is fond of animals, kill a cat
That was old and in pain with a blow from the edge of his palm.
He buried it in the garden, but I cannot remember its name.

Now the watchers are dispersing; the taxis drive away
Black in the black night. A huddle of people wait
Like mourners round the stage door. Is this what death is like?
For Violetta died after all. It is merely a ghost,
The voice gone, the beautiful dress removed, who steps in the rain.
Art, I conceive, is not so removed from life; for we look at death
Whether real or imagined from an impossible distance
And somewhere a final curtain is always descending.
The critics are already phoning their obituaries to the papers.
I do not think God is concerned with such trivial matters
But, father, though there will be no applause, die well.

DAY

Assembles day. Watch now
Who have not watched, how
It goes. Not as you thought,
Not at all. First, caught
As a child birthed in a caul,
Witness a dazed, struggling ball,
The sun. It has to fight
Up out of the ground, light
Diffused, not brilliant, grey.
Nevertheless it assembles day.

Now it puts it together bit by bit
Like a complex sentence, knit
By extravagant syntax. A tree
Untangles itself, breaks free
Of the dark, discovers green.
Nearby a pond has the sheen
Of an opal; its eye
Stares up at a reflected pond, the sky.
Olive grey at the edge, rushes
Stain the mauve blur of elder bushes.

Some of the dark does not rise;
Clouds go but the hill lies
Humped still. Now, sound
Falls in little spurts onto the ground
Out of the space above it, out of air;
Wings are not visible but birds are there.
With relentless beaks they peck the shawl
Of night to pieces. They let fall
Skein after skein; the rags
Drift in tatters where shadow lags.

You have been watching, but
You have not seen. Now shut
Your eyes again: night is back.
And how does day assemble from that black?
First, caught as a child. . . .
Already the conceit has you beguiled.
Very well, look! Take your hand
Away from your face. The land
Lies like a finished jigsaw. As an eyelash trembles,
As fast, as slow, day assembles.

WOULD'ST EAT A CROCODILE?

When I was a boy I occasionally lived in Africa,
Mostly in Summer on Sunday afternoons
When the assegais and the pampas grass
Stretched in an endless missionary-eating plain.

My eyes would squint in the heat, and the fever-swamps
Would draw one side of my face in a deadly ague.
At the height of the sun I would shout in delirium,
Staggering with thirst, but the pools were full of leeches.
Considering the number of tigers I killed
It is not surprising that in Africa they do not exist.

Remembering those days I am prompted to ask a question,
Though you need not answer it if you find it embarrassing.
It is this: have you ever been bitten by a crocodile?

I detect from your silence that slight unease of guilt
Which indicates your lack. It is an experience, believe me,
Not easily forgotten. But I blame no one but myself.
My bearers? I scorned such upperclass homosexual appendages!

No, Ladies and Gentlemen, even when you are indulging
In your most luxurious vices, such as hunting,
Or making love, reviling your relations, or merely
Listening, as one does, to Poetry, or Jazz, remember
You can live safely only one impossible life at a time.

But to return to my crocodile, my wound.
The day was exceptional and my genius ripe;
The plains of Africa glistened, only, remote in the azure sky,
The vultures hung, heavy with the digestible flesh of missionaries

Happily devoured, listening with the abrasive ecstasy of their kind
As I began with profound and reverent passion to play
The opening of the Beethoven piano sonata op. 111.

It was then that it happened. More terrible than vultures,
Out of a sky blue as the eyes of Mozart, the foul beast dived, and
SNAP! Ah, where was Beethoven then?

How long I lay there suffering in the grass I do not know,
Nor whether Stanley or Livingstone lifted my bleeding body
And stanched my wounds; it does not matter. But to this day I wish
I had known the name of that excellent crocodile,
My mentor and friend, most proper enemy.

I did not die, as I hope may be obvious;
But what of that beast? I have walked more warily since
In the Africa of my adulthood, in the feverish plains
Of London, through the assegai teeth of the world
Where missionaries smile, comforting as chocolate.

But sometimes, on an underground stairway, my wound throbs,
So that I lurch and clutch the rail that is always moving,
And the people disappearing forever into the past or the future
Are shocked, seeing those teethmarks red on my breast.

I do not want them to stop, with their righteous zeal
Offering words like lint and bandages, ambulances of concern.

As the crocodiles swarm in for the kill with their blazing eyes
And their teeth yellow as the keys of Beethoven's piano
Jangling on the plains of Africa, for what, Ladies and Gentlemen, must we call,
But for the terrible useless protection of God alone.

A FLORENTINE COMEDY

No doubt the peripatetic gazers
Think she is locked there in the too heavy frame:
Cranach's *Eve*. They stroll by and look,
Sucking their culture lolly, the boys in blazers
On an educational trip; but for her it is more than a game.
She fishes elsewhere and the catch jags on the hook.

Is it through the slant eye she slips inside?
When you look straight at her how she holds out
With that innocent gesture the fruit to the poor man
Beautiful and bewildered and sexless in his cage by her side.
Well, leave him there in his perpetual doubt;
We are talking about the woman.

The snake coils in her belly, while the seed
Flowers through her blood to the thorn tree of her hands:
She is spiked toward Christ's pitiless disaster.
Does the gangrenous head of Holofernes bleed
In the square with lust; or David where he stands
Freeze in the nauseous sweat of alabaster?

Some of the dust of angels where they fled
Powders her limbs with sacrilegious down;
She has sucked the tears of God to quick her eyes
Through which she views man's everlasting dead,
Their spent bones lodged in Hell's luxurious town
Drawn by desire of Satan's maculate prize.

I saw her once at midnight, naked and thin,
Like a mist over the Arno, and I could have smiled,
In the liberty of her sex meeting her on the prowl,
Save that, as she passed, from the agony of her sin
Reviling her sweet flesh lecherously reviled
I heard her sharp mouth like a vixen howl.

A SMALL CONSOLATION

The imperceptible units of decay
   Litter my rooms: echoes of words,
Holes of silences, bitterness
   Malevolent as weed in corners.

How many miles of pared
   Fingernails, of shed hair, and skin
Whose flakes, collected,
   Might bury me in my own dross?

Sometimes waking at night
   In darkness that is years of my closed eyes
I know that I lie
   Already stifled by layers of past self;

And I would cry out
   But griefs long since exhaled
Wash back from the walls, and I choke
   In a tide of stagnant, long-shed tears.

I am ordinary, and have been fearful of dying;
   But now I perceive
With a wry acceptance that so much of me has departed
   There is little left to suffer.

So I turn to sleep
   Under the adulterous wave of yawns and sighs
Already spent, consoled that thus I may exit
   Noiselessly, like a shadow, unnoticed through a small door.

Stevie Smith

I REMEMBER

It was my bridal night I remember,
An old man of seventy-three
I lay with my young bride in my arms,
A girl with t.b.
It was wartime, and overhead
The Germans were making a particularly heavy raid on
　　Hampstead.
What rendered the confusion worse, perversely
Our bombers had chosen that moment to set out for Germany.
Harry, do they ever collide?
I do not think it has ever happened,
Oh my bride, my bride.

THE JUNGLE HUSBAND

Dearest Evelyn, I often think of you
Out with the guns in the jungle stew
Yesterday I hittapotamus
I put the measurements down for you but they got lost in the
　　fuss
It's not a good thing to drink out here
You know, I've practically given it up dear.
Tomorrow I am going alone a long way
Into the jungle. It is all grey
But green on top
Only sometimes when a tree has fallen
The sun comes down plop, it is quite appalling.
You never want to go in a jungle pool
In the hot sun, it would be the act of a fool
Because it's always full of anacondas, Evelyn, not looking ill-
　　fed
I'll say. So no more now, from your loving husband, Wilfred.

THOUGHTS ABOUT THE PERSON FROM PORLOCK

Coleridge received the Person from Porlock
And ever after called him a curse,
Then why did he hurry to let him in?
He could have hid in the house.

It was not right of Coleridge in fact it was wrong
(But often we all do wrong)
As the truth is I think he was already stuck
With Kubla Khan.

He was weeping and wailing: I am finished, finished,
I shall never write another word of it,
When along comes the Person from Porlock
And takes the blame for it.

It was not right, it was wrong,
But often we all do wrong.

May we enquire the name of the Person from Porlock?
Why, Porson, didn't you know?
He lived at the bottom of Porlock Hill
So had a long way to go,

He wasn't much in the social sense
Though his grandmother was a Warlock,
One of the Rutlandshire ones I fancy
And nothing to do with Porlock,

And he lived at the bottom of the hill as I said
And had a cat named Flo,
And had a cat named Flo.

I long for the Person from Porlock
To bring my thoughts to an end,
I am becoming impatient to see him
I think of him as a friend.

(*Thoughts About the Person from Porlock cont.*)

Often I look out of the window
Often I run to the gate
I think, He will come this evening,
I think it is rather late.

I am hungry to be interrupted
For ever and ever amen
O Person from Porlock come quickly
And bring my thoughts to an end.

I felicitate the people who have a Person from Porlock
To break up everything and throw it away
Because then there will be nothing to keep them
And they need not stay.

Why do they grumble so much?
He comes like a benison
They should be glad he has not forgotten them
They might have had to go on.

These thoughts are depressing I know. They are depressing,
I wish I was more cheerful, it is more pleasant,
Also it is a duty, we should smile as well as submitting
To the purpose of One Above who is experimenting
With various mixtures of human character which goes best,
All is interesting for him it is exciting, but not for us.
There I go again. Smile, smile, and get some work to do
Then you will be practically unconscious without positively
    having to go.

NOT WAVING BUT DROWNING

Nobody heard him, the dead man,
But still he lay moaning:
I was much further out than you thought
And not waving but drowning.

Poor chap, he always loved larking
And now he's dead
It must have been too cold for him his heart gave way,
They said.

Oh, no no no, it was too cold always
(Still the dead one lay moaning)
I was much too far out all my life
And not waving but drowning.

Nathaniel Tarn

THE LIFE WE DO NOT LEAD

The life we do not lead
looks down on us from both these banks and laughs
as Westminster delivers us into this tossing boat;

the life we do not lead
has the sleek hulls of ships moored to each bank
strange in our need as women and just as ignorant

of what they will put down;
the life we do not lead
keeps the sharp beaks of gulls to tear with and these wings

to beat itself to puffs of smoke in time for Charing Cross;
the life we do not lead
cannot be numbered as the Tower's stones

yet we evoke it corking down the Thames,
freezing in this late Spring, pretending Summer
smells somewhere like these boats—

What do I make of this, you know, our being bound,
bound by the life we really lead and down at heel
(our boots cold fudge where slippers tripped the Globe)

in Shakespeare's year, and pitch so thin in England?
From here ships sailed that bound the mummy world,
great spiders on the wind, their sails like spider webs

and held the huge Pacific in those sails
as I hoard all the dreams the spinner heart can weave—
the life we do not lead

shrinks to a matchbox tossed on a minor sewer
as we, led by the lives that part us, abdicate,
melting into a mush for fish who've never even seen the sea.

THE CURE

Among the rugosas and the wild, hip-loaded, feather-leaved,
thorn-warning ones it happened, not in the law-abiding beds.
Hip-orange and white the damned thing streaked, with a grey wash
in its mouth, and I knew, spat Oh God no and ran to the patch.
The whole bird racket in there had maelstromed and swirled out—
all that came back, jilted, as if drawn with stump paddles,
was a float that had not yet stained air with the softest of greys.
Had never begun. Seemed to be swimming, discovering, looking about.
With an idiot's sloth. The beak opening, closing, without a sound.
Saving was out because of that red bared spine and the thickening syrup
at the beak. Now I shall not kill a fly the size of a pinhead, no.
My hand could not find its way through the thorns and cat claws.
My feet came down on the early wings; they swam still, swam still.
A big fly lashed on to the gash and held tight. I stamped
again to dye the ground. The whole bird universe with its one
soul shuddered and winced, I know that: wings withered in my head.
What horror-struck, astonished wrath like mine, when I am gashed,
will hammer down its terrible extremities to comfort me?

THE WEDDING

The company of those I had flown all my life
surrounded me again as if I had homed to them,
migrated back on well-worn routes. Do we know
which of his haunts a bird prefers? A secretary-
bird, haughty with parrots, a snake-crusher,
grey in the coloured riot, I await the bride.
Who came, lilting like a paradise, all of white
haloed, preening a little, so proud in her
slow sailing up that aisle as in some eastern
garden she knew best. And was suddenly by me,
I terrified by her white arrival on my grey bough.
We sang not but were sung through the black
bobbing—crows: bowing and bobbing, hissing
their psalms over us, we: passive on our boughs.
Leant over and were pecked and bibbed by crossed
parental wings as if to imprint and perpetuate
our "instinct" for the nest. And then a glass,
like a snake's eye, in a tray below. Trained,
I shivered it with the thud of a talon,
nearly destroyed the nest it seemed to me
in the silence, and cried out a loud sentence
meaning: I take you fowl of Jerusalem to wife.
And all that day, and that night, I sang them,
whose calls or territories I owned not, and to them,
before the break, was like a balm, a flowing
like the seas between their homes—in a trance
sang them in for the last time to my bough,
filled their mouths with morning praises of me simply.

THE RIGHTS OF MAN
"And goodbye to you too old rights-of-man!"

Marble blitzed with lightning contrast,
   skin's scarlet lining strung with green veins,
hard pearl in a soft oyster my finger plucks,
   music in layers on the silent air,

this is how I should lie in you if lie I do,
   this is how we should come together if at all,
only as Nature collates her impossibles,
   as dark says to light: I drink you, I eat you, Come!

but not: I am this, so, such and such/thus must make you
   this (etc.), not: I am not really I but only I,
you see, in this relation to you . . . and all this tedium
   when it has now been nightfall for so long.

You are astonished your art will not make marble whole,
   cry printer's ink over the rights of man.
I tell you inside out I'll not requite. There is no
   sea will welcome in this river where it flows.

BIOGRAPHICAL NOTES ON THE POETS

DANNIE ABSE, b. Cardiff, 1923. Has published five books of poems including *Tenants of the House* (1957), *Poems, Golders Green* (1962), and *A Small Desperation* (1968)—all Hutchinson. Other books include *Three Questor Plays* (Scorpion Press, 1968), *Ash on A Young Man's Sleeve* (an autobiographical novel, recently reissued by The Pergamon Press in their New English Library series), and a Vista paperback "Selection" of poems. Reads on the Argo L.P.s *Poetry and Jazz in Concert* (DA 26 & 27).

THOMAS BLACKBURN, b. Cumberland, 1916. His six published books of poems include *A Smell of Burning* (1961) and *A Breathing Space* (Putnam, 1964). Among his other publications are two books of criticism, *The Price of An Eye* (Longmans, 1961) and *Robert Browning* (Eyre and Spottiswoode, 1967), and an autobiographical work, *A Clip of Steel* (Macgibbon and Kee, 1969). Senior Lecturer in English at the College of St. Mark and St. John, Chelsea.

EDWIN BROCK, b. 1927. An ex-policeman, now working in advertising. Has published a novel and four books of poems: the most recent are *An Attempt at Exorcism* (1959) and *With Love From Judas* (Scorpion Press, 1963). A Selection of his poems appears in *Penguin Modern Poets No. 8*. Poetry editor of *Ambit*.

PETE BROWN, b. London, 1940. His first book of poems, *Few*, was published by the Migrant Press in 1966. Has three books due from Fulcrum Press: a small collection of poems entitled *Let 'em Roll Kafka!*, a *Collected Shorter Poems*, and an autobiography, *My Life with Pete Leibowitz*. Of late, has been writing lyrics for "The Cream".

ALAN BROWNJOHN, b. London, 1931. Read history at Oxford. Has been a parliamentary (Labour party) candidate, and now lectures at a College of Education. Publications include three volumes of poetry, *The Railings* (Digby Press, 1962), *The Lions' Mouths* (Macmillan, 1967), and *Sandgrains on a Tray* (1969). Appears in the *Penguin Modern Poets* series.

MICHAEL HAMBURGER. b. Berlin, 1924. Educated at Westminster School and Christ Church, Oxford. Formerly Reader in German at

Reading University. Has published a critical book, *Reason and Energy*, and English translations of Hölderlin, Brecht, Baudelaire, Hofmannsthal, and others. Co-editor of *Modern German Poetry, 1910–1960* and author of five books of poems. The most recent are *The Dual Site* (Longmans, 1958) and *Weather and Season* (Longmans, 1963). Appears in the *Penguin Modern Poets* series.

JOHN HEATH-STUBBS, b. London, 1918. Read English at Queen's College, Oxford. Has published eight books of poems since 1942. The most recent are *The Triumph of the Muse* (O.U.P., 1958) and *The Blue Fly in His Head* (O.U.P., 1962). His *Selected Poems* was published by The Oxford University Press in 1965. Co-editor of *The Faber Book of Twentieth-Century Verse*.

DOUGLAS HILL, b. Canada, 1935. Resident in Britain (on and off) since 1959. Poet, folklorist, historian. Has contributed poems, criticism, and reviews to many periodicals including *The Guardian*, *Tribune*, *Poetry Review*, and *Arts in Society* (U.S.A.). Editor of three science–fantasy anthologies. Co-author of *The Supernatural*; author of *The Opening of the Canadian West* (1967), and *John Keats* (1968). First collection in preparation.

ANSELM HOLLO, b. Helsinki, 1934. Resident in London since 1958. Translations include *Some Poems of Paul Klee* (Scorpion, 1962), *Red Cats* (City Lights, 1962), *Selected Poems of Andrei Voznesensky* (Grove Press, 1964), and *Selected Poems of Paavo Haavikko* (Cape, 1968). His own books of poems include *Faces and Forms* (Ambit, 1965), *And it's a Song* (Migrant, 1965), *Here We Go* (Stranger's Press, 1965), and *The Coherences* (Trigram Press, 1968). Visiting Professor at the Writer's Workshop, Univ. of Iowa, 1968–9.

TED HUGHES, b. Yorks., 1930. Author of three books of poems, *The Hawk in the Rain* (1957, Somerset Maugham Award), *Lupercal* (1960, Hawthornden Prize), and *Wodwo* (1967)—all Faber & Faber. Editor (with Thom Gunn) of *Five American Poets*, and author of five books for children.

BERNARD KOPS, b. London, 1926. Poet, playwright, novelist. Published plays include *The Hamlet of Stepney Green* (Penguin, 1959), *The Dream of Peter Mann* (Penguin, 1960), and *Four Plays* (Macgibbon and Kee, 1964). Other books include an autobiography, *The World is a Wedding* (Macgibbon and Kee, 1964), *Yes from No-Man's Land* and *The Dissent of Dominick Shapiro* (both novels, Macgibbon and Kee, 1965 & '66), and three books of poems, *Poems and Songs* (1958), *An Anemone for Antigone* (1959) and *Erica I Want to Read you Something* (1968)—all Scorpion Press.

138   Biographical Notes on the Poets

LAURIE LEE, b. Glous., 1914. Author of the best-selling autobiographical novel *Cider with Rosie*, a travel book on Spain, *A Rose for Winter*, and three books of poems: *Bloom of Candles* (John Lehmann, 1947), *The Voyage of Magellan* (verse-drama for radio, 1948), and *The Sun My Monument* (Chatto and Windus, 1954 and 1961). A Selection of his poems appears in the Vista Books Pocket Poets series. Reads on the Argo L.P.s *Poetry and Jazz in Concert*.

CHRISTOPHER LOGUE, b. 1926. Books of poems include *Wand and Quadrant* (1953), *First Testament* (1954), *The Weekdream Sonnets* (1955), *Songs* (Hutchinson, 1959), *Patrocleia* (Scorpion, 1962), and *Pax* (Rapp and Carroll, 1967). Plays include *Songs from the Lillywhite Boys* (Scorpion, 1960) and *Antigone* (1961). Records include Poets Reading No. 3 (Jupiter), *Red Bird* (Poetry and Jazz, Parlaphone), *The Death of Patrolclus* (77 Records).

SPIKE MILLIGAN, b. India, 1918. Wrote, nurtured, and appeared in *The Goon Show* from its beginnings in 1951. Won TV Producers' and Directors' "Writer of the Year" award following TV series *A Show Called Fred* and *Son of Fred*, 1956 and '57. His two most successful West End plays were *The Bed-Sittingroom* and *Oblomov*. Author of a novel, *Puckoon* (Blond, 1963) and several books of childrens' and nonsense verse including *Silly Verse for Kids* (Dobson, 1959), *A Dustbin of Milligan* (1961), and *The Little Pot Boiler* (1966).

ADRIAN MITCHELL, b. London, 1932. Edited *Isis* and *Oxford Poetry*, 1955. Has held a number of top journalistic jobs. His publications include a novel, *If You See Me Comin'* (1962) and two books of poems, *Poems* (1964) and *Out Loud* (Cape, 1968). Did the English stage adaption for the Aldwych production of *The Marat Sade*. Reads on the Argo L.P.s *Poetry and Jazz in Concert*.

DOM MORAES, b. India, 1938. Has lived in London since coming down from Oxford in 1959. Author of three books of poems, *A Beginning* (Parton Press, 1957), *Poems* (1960), and *John Nobody* (Eyre and Spottiswoode, 1965). Represented in *Penguin Modern Poets No. 2*. Has recently published an autobiographical book *My Son's Father*.

PETER PORTER, b. Australia, 1929. Has published three books of poems, *Once Bitten, Twice Bitten* (1961), *Poems Ancient and Modern* (1964), and *A Porter Folio* (Scorpion Press, 1969). Represented in *Penguin Modern Poets No. 2*. Lives in London, and is currently the *New Statesman* radio critic.

Biographical Notes on the Poets 139

JEREMY ROBSON, b. N. Wales, 1939. The *Tribune* poetry critic and originator of *Poetry and Jazz in Concert*. First book, *Thirty-Three Poems*, published by Sidgwick and Jackson in 1964. Edited *An Anthology of Young British Poets* (P.V., 1968). Reads on an Argo E.P. *Before Night/Day* (EAF 115) and on the Argo L.P.s *Poetry and Jazz in Concert*. Lives in London, and works as an editor for Aldus Books.

VERNON SCANNELL, b. Lincs., 1922. Served during World War II with the Gordon Highlanders in N. Africa and Normandy. Once a professional boxer. He is a frequent broadcaster and has written dramatic features in verse for the Third Programme. His novels include *The Fight, The Face of The Enemy*, and *The Dividing Night*; and his books of poems *A Mortal Pitch, Masks of Love* (Heinemann Award for Literature, 1960), *A Sense of Danger*, and *Walking Wounded* (Eyre and Spottiswoode, 1965).

JON SILKIN, b. London, 1930. Gregory Fellow in Poetry at Leeds University from 1958–60. Editor of the literary quarterly, *Stand*. Has published five books of poems, *The Peaceable Kingdom, The Two Freedoms, The Reordering of the Stones, Nature with Man*, and *New and Selected poems* (published by Chatto and Windus in 1966). In 1968, Northern House published a pamphlet of his translations from the Israeli poet Natan Zach, *Against Parting*.

JOHN SMITH, b. Bucks., 1924. Formerly editor of *The Poetry Review*, and editor of a number of anthologies including *The Pattern of Poetry* and *My Kind of Verse*. His six published volumes of poetry include *The Dark Side of Love* (1952), *The Birth of Venus, Excursus in Autumn* (1958, Poetry Book Society Choice), *A Letter to Lao Tze* (1961), and *A Discreet Immorality* (Hart-Davies, 1965).

STEVIE SMITH, b. Hull. She has written criticism for most of the leading weeklies. Her publications include *Novel on Yellow Paper, Over the Frontier*, and *The Holiday* (novels); *A Good Time Was Had By All, Tender Only to One, Mother, What is Man?, Harold's Leap* (poems); *Not Waving but Drowning* (poems and drawings, Deutsch, 1957); also *Cats in Colour* and *Some Are More Human Than Others* (sketch-books). Her *Selected Poems* was published by Longmans in 1962, and *The Frog Prince and Other Poems* in 1966. Appears in *Penguin Modern Poets No. 8*.

NATHANIEL TARN, b. Paris, 1928. Has published two books of poetry, *Old Savage/Young City* (1964) and *Where Babylon Ends* (Cape, 1968); also a translation of Pablo Neruda's long poem, *The Heights of Macchu Picchu* (Cape, 1966). Represented in *Penguin Modern Poets No. 7*. Editor of the Cape Golliard Editions. Lives in London.

APPENDIX

A selected list of concerts given between
February 1961 and June 1969.

1961
Saturday, February 4th	*Hampstead Town Hall*
Sunday, June 11th	*Royal Festival Hall*

1962
Sunday, February 25th	*Belgrade Theatre, Coventry*
Sunday, April 8th	*Cheltenham Town Hall*
Saturday, May 5th	*Oxford Town Hall*
Sunday, July 15th	*Hintlesham Arts Festival (Hintlesham Hall)*
Sunday, September 9th	*Birmingham Arts Festival (Town Hall)*
Thursday, September 13th	*Wellingborough (Centre 42 Festival)*
Thursday, September 27th	*Nottingham (Centre 42 Festival)*
Thursday, October 11th	*Leicester (Centre 42 Festival)*
Thursday, October 25th	*Birmingham (Centre 42 Festival)*
Thursday, November 8th	*Bristol (Centre 42 Festival)*
Thursday, November 22nd	*Hayes (Centre 42 Festival)*
Saturday, December 8th	*Wood Green Council Chamber*

1963
Sunday, January 13th	*Prince of Wales Theatre, Cardiff (Welsh Arts Council)*
Saturday, January 19th	*King's Hall, Hackney*
Sunday, February 3rd	*Royal Court Theatre*
Sunday, March 1st	*St. Pancras Arts Festival*
Monday, April 22nd	*Hampstead Theatre Club*
Friday, May 3rd	*Bromsgrove Arts Festival*
Sunday, May 19th	*Victoria Theatre, Stoke-on-Trent*
Tuesday, May 21st	*Oxfam Charity Concert (Hampstead Town Hall)*
Monday, June 10th	*Decca Recording Studios ("Live" concert to record the two Argo L.P.s Poetry and Jazz in Concert—DA 26 & 27)*

Appendix 141

Sunday, July 7th	*Elmhurst Theatre, Camberley*
Monday, October 7th	*Maidenhead Music Society*
Tuesday, October 15th	*Bath Music Society*
Thursday, October 31st	*The Midland Institute, Birmingham (Centre 42)*
Thursday, November 7th	*Wellingborough Technical College (Centre 42)*
Sunday, November 17th	*Colston Hall, Bristol (Centre 42)*
Friday, November 22nd–Sunday, November 24th	*Welsh Arts Council Tour:* *King's Hall, Aberystwyth (Friday); Brangwyn Hall, Swansea (Saturday); New Theatre, Cardiff (Sunday)*
Friday, November 29th	*Community Centre, Hayes (Centre 42)*
Friday, December 13th	*Wood Green Council Chamber*
Tuesday, December 24th	*Aldus Books, London*

1964

Sunday, January 12th	*Phoenix Theatre, Leicester (Centre 42—two concerts)*
Friday, January 24th	*Civic Centre, Nottingham (Centre 42)*
Thursday, February 27th	*Chelsea College of Science and Technology*
Sunday, March 3rd	*St. Pancras Arts Festival (Town Hall)*
Thursday, April 16th	*Charity Concert (St. Pancras Town Hall)*
Wednesday, May 6th	*South-West Technical College, Walthamstow*
Sunday, September 20th	*Queen's Theatre, Hornchurch*
Sunday, November 15th	*Theatre Royal, Stratford East*
Sunday, November 29th	*Ben-Uri Art Gallery*
Friday, December 18th	*Wood Green Council Chamber*

1965

Saturday, January 2nd	*King's Hall, Hackney*
Friday, January 8th	*High School, Hessle (E. Yorks)*
Sunday, January 17th	*Arts Theatre, Cambridge*
Monday, January 18th	*Royal Academy of Art*
Sunday, March 7th	*Southampton University Arts Festival (Nuffield Theatre)*
Friday, March 19th	*Stafford Arts Festival*
Friday, March 26th	*Lambeth Arts Festival*

Appendix

Sunday, March 28th	*Theatre Royal, Stratford East*
Friday, April 2nd	*Camden School for Girls*
Wednesday, April 7th	*Elmhurst Theatre, Camberley*
Friday, April 30th	*Bristol University*
Sunday, May 9th	*Festival Theatre, Chichester*
Saturday, May 29th	*College of St. Mark and St. John, Chelsea*
Monday, May 31st	*Hampstead Arts Festival (Blackfriars Hall)*
Saturday, June 12th	*Civic Theatre, Scunthorpe*
Tuesday, July 13th	*Sutton High School*
Friday, September 10th	*Theatre Royal, Stratford East*
Friday, November 12th	*Southampton University*
Monday, November 15th	*Belfast Arts Festival (Queen's College)*
Saturday, November 20th	*Gerrard's Cross Music Society*
Friday, December 10th	*The Poetry Society*

1966

Tuesday, February 15th	*High School, Hessle (afternoon), Regional College of Arts and Crafts, Hull*
Friday, February 18th	*Birmingham College of Advanced Technology*
Saturday, February 19th	*White Hart Lane (New School) Harringay*
Friday, March 11th	*Southampton University*
Sunday, May 8th	*Cheshunt Town Hall*
Friday, May 13th	*Havering Arts Festival (Romford Central Library)*
Saturday, May 21st	*Birmingham University*
Friday, June 10th	*Hitchin College of Further Education*
Friday, June 17th	*Cwmbran (Arts Association)*
Friday, June 24th and Saturday, June 25th	*New Universities Festival (Keele)*
Sunday, June 26th	*Victoria Theatre, Stoke-on-Trent*
Wednesday, June 29th	*Ludlow Arts Festival*
Thursday, July 21st	*Harlow Arts Festival,*
Thursday, October 27th	*St. Pancras Town Hall*
Saturday, November 19th	*Kent University*
Friday, November 27th	*David Lister High School, Hull (afternoon); Hull University*
Monday, December 5th	*Chelmsford Civic Theatre*
Saturday, December 10th	*Barnet College*
Tuesday, December 20th	*The Highwayman, Camberley*

Appendix 143

1967

Saturday, February 4th and Sunday, February 5th	*Reardon Smith Lecture Theatre, Cardiff (Welsh Arts Council)*
Sunday, February 6th	*Institute of Education*
Saturday, February 18th	*Hornsey Town Hall (Harringay Council)*
Saturday, February 25th	*University of N. Wales Festival, Bangor*
Saturday 4th March and Sunday 5th March	*Rolle College, Exmouth*
Friday, April 14th	*Hitchin College of Further Education*
Monday, April 17th– Saturday, April 22nd	*The Mayfair Theatre, London*
Thursday, April 27th	*Sutton High School*
Sunday, May 14th	*Lincoln Labour Party Festival*
Tuesday, June 6th	*The Highwayman, Camberley*
Friday, June 23rd	*Newham Arts Festival (Town Hall, Stratford E.)*
Sunday, June 25th	*Questors Theatre, Ealing*
Friday, June 30th	*Angry Arts Festival (The Round House)*
Friday, July 7th	*Ludlow Arts Festival*
Wednesday, July 19th	*Bryanston School Festival, Blandford*
Wednesday, October 11th	*Havering Arts Festival (Romford Central Library)*
Sunday, October 29th	*International Students' House*
Sunday, November 19th	*Belgrade Theatre, Coventry*

1968

Sunday, January 21st	*Arts Theatre, Cambridge*
Friday, January 26th	*Wye College of Agriculture*
Saturday, January 27th	*Barnet College*
Tuesday, February 6th	*Institute of Education*
Sunday, March 3rd	*International Students' House*
Sunday, March 10th	*Southampton University Festival*
Saturday, March 16th	*College of Education, Hereford*
Friday, May 3rd	*College of Education, Eastbourne*
Sunday, May 5th	*Keele University Festival (Victoria Theatre)*
Thursday, June 13th	*Sussex University*
Sunday, June 30th	*Festival Theatre, Malvern*
Wednesday, July 3rd	*Westminster Medical School (Students') Festival*
Sunday, September 15th	*New Theatre, Cardiff*
Friday, September 27th	*High School, Hessle*
Sunday, October 12th	*Malvern Girls' College (Recorded by the BBC)*

Sunday, October 27th	*Elmhurst Theatre, Camberley*
Sunday, November 17th	*Arts Theatre, Cambridge*
Wednesday, November 20th	*Sussex University*
Friday, November 22nd	*Hitchin College of Further Education*
Thursday, November 28th	*University of Surrey Festival (Battersea Town Hall)*
Sunday, December 1st	*Wye College*
Sunday, December 8th	*University of Surrey Festival (Guildford Civic Hall)*

1969

Friday, January 10th	*BBC Third Programme:* Poetry and Jazz in Concert, *from Malvern Girls' College (producer George MacBeth)*
Saturday, January 25th	*Institute of Contemporary Arts, London*
Thursday, January 30th	*Holborn Library*
Thursday, February 6th	*Chalk Farm Library*
Saturday, February 15th	*Enfield County School*
Sunday, March 2nd	*Hull University*
Thursday, March 13th	*Madely College, Stafford*
Friday, March 14th	*Hereford College of Education*
Saturday, March 15th	*Cardiff University*
Monday, April 21st	*Southampton University*
Monday, May 12th	*Camden Arts Festival*
Sunday, June 22nd	*Queen Elizabeth Hall (presented and recorded by Argo for future release on L.P.)*

The Musicians

The musicians for the first two concerts were assembled and led by Arnon Ben-Tovim. Since then Michael Garrick has written and arranged all the music for the concerts, including settings of poems. Apart from leading his own trio and sextet (in, and outside, the concerts) he is now pianist with the distinguished Rendell/Carr Quintet. As a result, this Quintet—playing Garrick's music, under his direction—has become closely linked with Poetry and Jazz in Concert.

Individual musicians who have featured prominently over the years are:

Piano: Michael Garrick
Reeds: Joe Hariott, Tony Coe, Don Rendell
Horns: Shake Keane, Ian Carr
Drums: Colin Barnes, Trevor Tomkins
Bass: Jeff Clyne, Coleridge Goode, John Taylor, Dave Green